CO

D1034757

SAINT MARY'S
COMMUNITY COLLEGE LIBRARY

HOPE
IS THE REMEDY

HOPE IS THE REMEDY

Bernard Häring, C.Ss.R.

DOUBLEDAY & COMPANY, INC., GARDEN CITY, NEW YORK
1972

Library of Congress Catalog Card Number 72–76165
Copyright © 1971, 1972 by Bernard Häring
All Rights Reserved
Printed in the United States of America

CONTENTS

HOPE
IS THE REMEDY

PREFACE

The years following Vatican Council II have provided ample evidence that *hope* is the distinctive password of the secular world and of the People of God in this era of rapid change, of illusions and disillusions. What the world expects from the People of God is above all a realistic message of hope, the courage to be and to live in the midst of the pangs of childbirth with a hope that gives new life.

The undreamed-of progress of modern science and technology have awakened new expectations which go beyond neoteric technical possibilities or scientific verification. It is a whole sensation of a flood tide in progress and development, a sensation of hope in the total life style of a generation. The men of today keep a sharp lookout for totally new ways of investing their energies in the shaping of history and of their immediate environment, but in this new expectation, there are contingent forces of tension and frustration. After the destruction of two world wars, humanity hoped for peace; it is now shocked by the explosions of violence which rock their cherished dream.

Aggravation of the drug-addiction problem and widespread awareness of increasing environmental pollution are but two symbols of a new human experience of hopelessness and frustration. Man is now confronted with new problems resulting from earlier hopes which would be better termed *illusions*. Humanity today is both torn and shaken by the sensational hopes of yesterday and wallowing in a sea of anxiety neuroses.

How will modern man react if his noblest hopes seem destined to oblivion in this new age of anguish and neurosis while his capacity in the technological fields and in the pragmatic sciences keeps unfolding at a geometric rate? Will he, out of existential despair, devote all his energies to technology and its supportive sciences? The hippie movement represents a protest against just such a decision. Hippies fear the emptiness of a world in which man's best efforts are expended for external progress while man as man seems to have renounced personal growth. In final analysis, is not the radicalism of this kind of protest a sign that mankind never relinquishes the hope of becoming more humane? In essence, hippiedom indicates that man will abandon many other hopes while clinging to his most existential yearning. However, Christian hope inspires a more healthy protest and a more effective remedy.

The renewal efforts in the Church, the ecumenical, biblical and liturgical movements, the awakening of the laity to responsible service in the Church and society, the ideas Pope John XXIII embodied so uniquely and the courage of Vatican II to embark on an uncertain future, were not these things, for many of us, much more than a sensation of hope? They represented more than we had dared hope to see realized in our lifetime. In response, we can fittingly render thanks and honor God only if we hope for still greater things.

In these well-founded hopes, grounded in the visible signs of God's gracious presence, we have somewhat of a tonal scale of modern man's desires. At the very core of his life is tension between the hopes raised by one particular field of endeavor and the danger of despair generated by other perhaps more important tasks; there is tension in the imbalance between the new experience of power on the one hand and greater awareness of human limitations and frustrations on the other. Much sand has been thrown into the mill of renewal by the very mixture of these hopes and by technical man's impatient eagerness to construct things which cannot be refashioned at technology's actual pace. Large bodies move slowly and the Church is no exception to this physical law; therefore, ensuing discontent and disillusionment are evident in many parts of the world.

The innumerable underground churches which have sprung up in all parts of the world parallel the hippie reaction to this situation within the Church. The movement mirrors the many-faceted hopes and illusions of modern man. Unfortunately, the label of "underground churches" is also applied to valid groups exemplifying spontaneity and endurance in creative suffering whereas others are no more than a grumbling Church in sterile reaction against disgruntled reactionaries. It is my conviction, however, that on the whole the element of creativity which prevails in such groups is an effective sign of hope.

At first glance, it may seem at times that pessimism is more prevalent than hope. Two very different and opposing groups help to promote this mistaken impression. One need only scan the reactions to Pope Paul VI's utterances, decisions and actions. Even when his message, on the whole, is an appeal to courage and trust, there are cynics who quote only his expressions of concern,

grief and despair; they seem attuned only to the pessimistic overtones. It may be that these people need a
scapegoat for their own anguish and lack the courage to
face up to this reality. They are angry because history
has not set its seal on their hopes. The reforms they
wanted and the speed they had opted for failed to
materialize.

Others have dwelt on the pessimistic undertones of the
papal pronouncements because of their own masochistic
tendencies and need to dwell on gloom and despair.
They wish to canonize their anxiety neurosis. The existential fear prompting their despondency is their futile search
for liberation from the duty of committing themselves to
salvific change.

However these two vocal groups are not representative
of the whole world nor of the whole Church. Hope is
not dead; on the contrary, hope is finding new classical
modes of expression. I shall mention two examples only.
The astronauts, who with almost incredible skill and
courage have opened new vistas of technical progress
and human valor have also, in the midst of their successful
exploits, openly proclaimed to the whole of mankind
their praise of the Creator. This represents a new awareness of the continued presence of God in an ongoing
creation. Similarly Pope Paul's pilgrimages have shown
undaunted courage, by-passing so many traditions and
twice visiting in the Orient the leader of the Orthodox
Churches before inviting him to a visit in Rome. Whatever may be said critically of Pope Paul's journeys, are
they not symbolic of the pilgrim Church setting out for
new horizons in constant hope?

Other strong indications of hope are the results of the
most comprehensive survey ever made in the field of religious sociology, conducted recently in West Germany in
preparation for the country's great Pastoral Council. It

yielded very interesting insights as to prevalent anxieties, concerns and hopes. Some 4,400,000 Germans completed and returned the questionnaire. Interesting and striking was the fact that personal concerns and anxieties were very secondary. Some 44.2 per cent expressed worry over the uncertainty of the future of mankind and of their own future as opposed to 66.9 per cent who indicated an overriding concern for peace. The 44.2 per cent quoted above were included in the 55.1 per cent who expressed personal uneasiness that in spite of all our technological advances, a considerable segment of mankind is still suffering from starvation and poverty. Some 44.6 per cent were worried about the difficulties of initiating a dialogue between the older and younger generations. Altogether, these concerns fail to meet the diagnostic requirements of an anxiety neurosis. On the contrary, they are healthy signs that the man of today evinces a responsible attitude toward the great tasks confronting humanity.

For about 20.4 per cent only did the ecumenical movement with all its attendant changes constitute any source of anxiety; the great majority approved of the ecumenical initiatives of the Catholic Church. Some 46.4 per cent of the respondents were convinced that the Catholic Church should be even more daring and courageous in striving toward Christian unity.

When asked about the tasks of the Church, only a relatively small percentage inclined toward some form of religious individualism. The great majority of respondents expected the Church to be a prophetic voice in the world on behalf of social justice and the development of peoples, while not neglecting the specifically religious task of honoring and praising God and proclaiming the message of salvation. The over-all picture is one of a people searching for an integrated hope.

One is justified in asking: how representative was the

4,400,000 sample with respect to the 18,000,000 total to whom the questionnaire was distributed? Admittedly, the regular churchgoers were overrepresented. It was therefore deemed advisable to sample for representativeness of the whole West German population. The picture which emerged was essentially the same; however, it seems that among regular churchgoers and those admitting to a positive rapport with the Church, hope and social concern figured more prominently.

Convinced that hope is one of the great existential themes of this decade, for the past two years I have accepted invitations for lectures and conferences that focused primarily on the topic of hope. The discussions which followed the lectures have helped me grasp better the complex existential reality of the theme. The book now presented to the public arose mainly from a workshop I conducted for more than seven hundred religious teachers: laymen, priests and religious at Holy Name College in Oakland, California, in August 1970 and the lecture series which I gave at the International Catechetical Institute in London, Ontario, in September 1970. I have decided to publish my remarks because of insistent appeals from the participants. However, I would never have found the time and courage to do so without the most generous collaboration of Sister Gabrielle L. Jean who devoted part of her sabbatical year to the transcription of the lectures from tapes, to editing and re-editing them after common reflection. I wish to express to her my profound gratitude.

Bernard Häring, C.Ss.R.

December 10, 1970
Rome

1
UNMASKING THE ENEMY

The science of catechetics has to explore a great variety of literary genres and since catechists presently find themselves involved in the process of demythologization, I would like to begin with a myth or legend about skunks. Obviously, the very nature of the narrative reveals its imaginary character; nevertheless, it can serve to convey a truth likely to be confirmed in the light of personal experience.

Toward the end of the Council, I had a "vision" in which my olfactory sense came prominently into play. Before me I saw a great assembly, the Universal Congress of Skunks. Presiding at the opening session was the Supervisor of Devils, the Super-Skunk, who addressed his fellow skunks in the following manner:

Dear beloved and truly abominable skunks,

Over the past few months and years, you have been doing very poorly in terms of stinking and radiating frustration around you. You seem unable to cope with the challenge of that old guy, John XXIII, who should have died some years earlier instead of spreading optimism about the

world contaminating even the secular segment and people
outside his fold. But now, dearly beloved and equally hated
devils, the Grand Council is proposing a new unified strategy, the goal of which is nothing less than the transformation
of the Church, our strong enemy, into a perfect sacrament of
pessimism, a truly visible and effective sign of our infernal
odor. For this task, muster into service whatever gray matter
you have at your disposal. Learn from modern psychology
that there are no longer specific heresies worth opposing
nor any well-defined fears; use the pervasive force of anxiety.
Anguish and anxiety must prevail: an anguished pope,
apprehensive bishops, anxious religious superiors, overly
concerned liberals, nervous theologians, worried canonists—
anxiety and *anguish* are now the passwords; let them be a
universal phenomenon.

The second part of our strategy pertains to the proper
mixture of ingredients. American chemists have much to
teach us about our prized totem; they combine our skunk's
extract with other elements as a basic ingredient which gives
perfumes a quality of permanence, the kind much coveted
by sophisticated ladies desirous of flowery fragrance.

So far, you stupid devils have offered the whole world
nothing but naked pessimism which is no longer a market-
able product. You must concoct a more effective mixture as
suggested by today's chemists. Do not be afraid to speak out
with unctuous piety and with great concern for orthodoxy
and progress but always include "skunk extract" as the
basic element. Use this ingredient in such a way that our
infernal odor of pessimism remains always detectable in
the final product. Try it in all forms and combinations. No
longer will you need to resort to violent attacks on God and
religion; try the "God-is-dead" theology as one tactic. For
those who claim he is alive in the shrine of unchanging
words, formulas and rituals, it is of the utmost importance
for you to deliver carefully and effectively the message
that God is well preserved in that tomb and will never rise
again. Encourage people to talk about the hopeless absence
of God on the one hand and make a concerted effort to

speak to the People of God in a dead language; the out-
come will be the same.

Inspire prominent churchmen to focus their attention and
devote all their energies to those truths that are irrelevant,
for instance, the number of choirs of angels or whether
angels are purely material or spiritual beings, or both. Help
them escape from their narrow world to a lofty idealism.
Keep them involved in lengthy theoretical arguments about
hypothetical situations; manage especially to distract their
attention from concern about such foolish things as love and
justice in the world.

Availing yourselves of all your gifts of oratory, preach faith
but let it be a faith without hope, consisting of formulas, a
mere catalogue of things or beliefs; this will be one of our
new gimmicks. Let them fight tooth and nail about "tran-
substantiation" or other sacred words far removed from the
interests of the people. Help them translate the expression
"Church authority" as "those who take the place of God";
what better way is there of successfully driving God out of
the world? When such people happen to be cardinals, bishops or religious superiors, there seems to be no better way
of maneuvering God out of the world. Arouse their anger if
someone resists them or views natural law differently or
holds an opinion different from theirs. Let them suspend,
silence or "transfer" all those priests who display a sensi-
tivity to people's needs. Allow them to cry out: "My authority! What I say is God's word!" Then proceed to confuse the
people by saying: "This is the Magisterium." Assist those
brave cardinals who think they are promoting salvation by
prescribing styles of dress for religious women. Whet the
interest of the entire People of God: lay, religious and cleric,
in progress but confuse them about the meaning of it;
incite them to impatience if progress does not come about
quickly enough, making them angry and bitter.

Devote considerable attention to progressives, encour-
aging them to expend at least 90 per cent of their energy
on fighting conservatives, whether they be bishops, theologians, canonists, nuns or other holy people. Teach every-

body to pray along with Charles de Gaulle at Mont-
martre: "Sacred Heart of Jesus, trust in me!" Tell believers
to have faith in themselves; let them forget the grace of
God—a dangerous concept for us. Rally the truly strong believers; lead them to believe in their own miracles. Suggest
that they use drugs if need be to produce visions, appari-
tions and wonders. Make sure that their miracles in no way
resemble those performed by our Enemy who relieved the
poor, cured the sick and fed the hungry; such tendencies
must be rooted out completely.

Single out for greater attention all the marginal religious
issues you can think of, such as the Churches arguing among
themselves about the validity of certain successful marriages.
Let the pastors teach and stress the idea that only those
marriages are sacraments or valid which are performed
according to prescribed ceremonies and Church laws. Fan
the flames of discussion about these matters; this tactic will
divert pastors from concern about stabilizing marriages or
educating spouses in that love our Enemy taught.

Next, beloved and stinking friends, tell them more about
freedom; this is our specific business. We have to enlighten
the world about the notions of self-determination and self-
fulfillment. Each person must be brought to focus on his
own freedom and become oblivious of the freedom of
others. If this freedom is not immediately forthcoming, get
them to indulge in self-pity and anger. Offer your pro-
posals in a very pious and attractive way in apparent good
faith, but maintain the fundamental thrust in pessimism.

Do not relent in your efforts to preserve the Latin language and other similar archaic tokens; adopt *Una Voce* as
your battle cry. Be especially careful to see that prayer
formulas remain always and everywhere the same. Encourage pious people to pray and pray, for hours on end; let
them use only the old formulas in the belief that the latter
will be all the more effective if duly counted and recorded.
As for others, you have to teach them how to get God to do
their bidding. Now that indulgences are no longer attractive,

teach them self-indulgence, self-pity and similar forms of secular prayer.

Blind people to the merits of their opponents. Conservatives must call liberals "hopeless cases" and older folks must do the same with youth. Teach conservatives, regressives, progressives and liberals equally how to fight for progress and Church renewal; it is especially important that they oppose and attack each other mercilessly.

Present the institutional Church as an object for constant criticism but keep constructive ideas out of the business. Urge your adherents to be sharply critical of the Church, of priests, of those who rule as well as those who are ruled. Do not allow people to believe that "totem hunting" is dead. You know that totem hunters were warriors who introduced wild aggressiveness into the world. The time is now ripe for more totem hunting: critics criticizing critics, one group disparaging the other.

Let priests and nuns talk day and night about optional celibacy, but rightly understood as optional fidelity. Help them bring about the Association for Pastoral Renewal with its stated goal: to reveal to the whole world how miserable frustrated priests can be when they are expected to keep their promises. Confuse the issue as much as you can.

Make a great show of conservatives whose charism is to frustrate progressives. Incite progressives to display even more bitterness than those already frustrated by reforms. In all this be utterly shameless; claim that you are acting in the best interests of religion or faith or piety; you will then have a potent mixture at your disposal.

Piously insist on the observance of all commandments, save that of love and mercy. In the past, you did marvelously well with rigorism and Jansenism but the present age calls for a new approach. Be wary of any method advocating love and concern for other people. Be voluble about Christian hope but avoid any mention of Christ's death and resurrection as the basis of hope. Never bring into play such old-fashioned notions as self-denial; speak only about an easily

accessible hope, a man-made hope, a secular hope for
earthly progress.

Do not tolerate a sense of humor for it could be fatal
because of its relationship to humility; present humor solely
as a waste of time. Encourage only a futile optimism based
on secular achievements or pietistic magic. This is an unfail-
ing way of enlisting recruits for our pessimistic sect.

Remember that our goal is to transform the Church of
our Enemy into a sacrament of pessimism. Therefore, place
daily on the desk of the pope a long list of sad events for
his information; do the same with bishops, religious superiors and everyone not now belonging to our group. Be
fearless in combining the various pious elements provided
you include always the basic and the most potent ingredient
of stinking pessimism.

The Supervisor of Devils rambled on for some time in
the same vein; at the end of his great oration, all the
grown skunks mumbled a pious "Amen!" and set out de-
terminedly to implement the new unified strategy.

Are we post-conciliar Christians to be victims of this
demonic strategy or will we say a firm "No! Begone,
Satan!"? It no longer matters whether we wear the label
of conservative or liberal; what truly matters is that we
place our trust in Christ and that we act as men and
women filled with divine hope and not with trust in ourselves.

2
CHRIST OUR HOPE

Pierre Teilhard de Chardin was fond of repeating: "The world belongs to those who offer it the greater hope." What is offered to us and that which we can offer the created universe is Christ, our hope. As long as we fail to present him to the world by our witness of faith, hope and love, others will be promising it greater hope. In our theological thinking as well as in our catechetical endeavors and in our lives, we must not allow anything to take the place of Christ nor conceal him who is truly our hope, our peace and our joy.

After first accepting Christ for ourselves, we must seek to offer the world the real Christ, the One who was, is and will come. There are too many caricatures of Christ presenting him as a sweet Jesus who disturbed no one, a Jesus of the Social Gospel limited to this worldly life. As Christians, our mission is to present Jesus as he offered himself to the world, as Christ our Savior and our hope.

Christ is our hope as the fulfillment of God's saving love, God's saving mercy and God's saving justice. He is our hope as the great sacrament, the great visible sign of God's fidelity and love for all men. Christ is our hope as victor over all evil powers, over frustration, over sin, over solidarity in sinfulness and selfishness, over anguish and death. Christ is our hope as the risen Lord; he is the new creation. He is the final Word of God to man, the last and final prophet promised to those who believe in him and are truly his disciples.

Jesus is the great and ever present reality in which our common history was and is completely anticipated in a personal event. In him are fulfilled all the past promises. All that was right, just and good in the ages before Christ's incarnation, death and resurrection was inspired by his grace and foreshadowed his coming in the flesh of this world, his death, resurrection, ascension and the mission of the Spirit who renews our heart, our mind and the face of the earth. Everything done throughout the ages with his grace bears the promise that he will complete the work in this history and beyond it. "The raising of Jesus to the status of Lord is a saving act of God which, at one point, turned the history which ended in his death into a fulfilled history. That is why it touches our own terrestrial history. . . . While the apocalyptic approach puts the eschaton at the end of the history of this world, Christianity has put it within history itself. . . . In the man Jesus the future of mankind has been revealed to us: the fulfillment of the life of Jesus himself, in both its individual and collective aspects."[1]

So Christ who died for us and was raised for us is a real event in human history. Yet, this is more than just a past historical event; it is an event that gives meaning and direction to all our hopes, to all past and future history. The final hope is already with us in Christ and through our faith in him. This is our understanding of hope in terms of Christian existentialism. The Christian commu-

[1] E. Schillebeeckx, O.P., "Some Thoughts on the Interpretation of Eschatology," *Concilium*, 41 (January 1969), 54.

nity that centers on "Christ is with us" is en route with
the pilgrim Church that trusts in him. However, Christ is
also present as Judgment already going on in the world.
Only if we accept him also as Judge over the sinful world,
over our selfish desires and the anguish caused by self-
concern and self-pity, only then do we truly receive him
as the Savior, our hope.

Christ is our hope through faith, but faith conceived
as an absolute readiness to listen to him, to treasure up
his words in our heart, meditating and acting upon
them. It is faith understood as a joyous, grateful acceptance of the One who is our Savior, our hope. It is through
faith that we, his people, entrust ourselves to him. We can
then hope everything from him, not in the manner of an
ancient rabbi who asked, "How do I get God to do my
will?" but rather according to the response he received
from the greater rabbi in the Talmud: "Entrust yourself
to God; conform your will to God's will and then God
will do your will." Hope, then, is a very existential act; it
implies entrusting ourselves to God in whatever he sends
us, even unexpectedly; thus we trust that he is with us as
our Savior and as our hope.

Christ is our hope if we are willing to become with him
and in him promoters of hope, symbols of promise, instruments of peace, signs of the shalom, of the peace that
has come in him. He is our hope if we entrust ourselves to
him for then we can conquer with him the powers of evil
and the great sins of despair, pessimism, anguish, self-
centeredness and self-indulgence.

Accepting Christ as our hope means that with him we
can even face death as a saving sign. Along with him, the
condemned One, we utter the final word of trust: "Father,
into thy hands I commit my spirit" (Lk. 23:46). If we
have received the sacraments of hope after having lived
accordingly and if we are conformed to Christ who has

died for us and risen for us, we can claim that true
Christian optimism so different from that easy optimism
suggested by the Supervisor of Devils. Christian optimism
is at its best when daily labor, hard work, the difficulties
of life, weakness, partial failure and contradiction assume new meaning in Christ, our hope, who died for us.

Christ is our hope by what he is, by what he says to us,
by his life and by his death and resurrection. Therefore,
the essential sign of Christian hope which distinguishes it
so radically from all other forms of hope is the Paschal
Mystery. Christian hope conquers the godless world, the
alienated world, when in faith we say "yes" to God's will,
the "yes" which puts to death our selfish desires. The
sacraments are signs of hope if, through living faith, they
are not just magic formulas but existential events, if they
open our heart and mind and will, our whole life, persons
and communities to the Paschal event of death and resurrection. Their reception, then, is a total opening and
surrender to Christ, our hope, so that we may become
ever more visibly and effectively signs of hope for the
world.

It will prove helpful to study some of the biblical texts
relating to hope, especially in the New Testament, the
great book of hope; we turn, for instance, to the Epistle
to the Romans for an optimistic outlook on salvation.
Some of the great thinkers of the past have advanced a
number of pessimistic theories, one of the most terrible
being the idea of an eternal limbo: billions and billions
of innocent children who, without any guilt on their part,
would have been relegated there forever and excluded
from the vision of God. Thus the misdeeds, the wrongdoing of Adam would have been out of proportion to salvation in Christ. "God's act of grace is out of proportion
to Adam's wrongdoing." It is obvious that each theory

must be tested against the background of this biblical teaching.

"God's act of grace is out of proportion to Adam's wrongdoing. For if the wrongdoing of one man brought death upon so many, its effect is vastly exceeded by the grace of God and the gift that came to so many by the grace of the one man, Jesus Christ. And again, the gift of God is not to be compared in its effect with that one man's sin; for the judicial action, following upon the one offence, issued in a verdict of condemnation, but the act of grace, following upon so many misdeeds, issued in a verdict of acquittal. For if by the wrongdoing of that one man death established its reign, through a single sinner, much more shall those who receive in far greater measure God's grace and his gift of righteousness, live and reign through the One Man, Jesus Christ" (Rom. 5:15-17). The whole theology of St. Paul is a hymn praising God's grace. "It follows, then, that as the issue of one misdeed was condemnation for all men, so the issue of one just act is acquittal and life for all men. For as through the disobedience of the one man many were made sinners, so through the obedience of the one man many will be made righteous" (Rom. 5:18-19).

This hope is not offered to man magically. If the sinfulness of mankind "in Adam" is a fate with which everyone has to contend, each can be freed in Christ but only if we accept Christ as he is, as the Father revealed him, Christ as the bearer of the burdens of all men. We must restore to the Christian sacraments the sacraments of faith, the full character of hope, namely, of entrusting ourselves to the Father in the manner of Christ. St. Paul explains it well: "By baptism we were buried with him, and lay dead, in order that, as Christ was raised from the dead in the splendor of the Father, so also we might set our feet upon the new path of life" (Rom. 6:4). So it is

through God's precious offer, through God's commitment
to us, through the fulfillment of his promises to us that we
set our feet upon the new path of life by living according
to faith and grace.

Christian hope is a gift, an undeserved gift of peace,
but it is also a call to decision, to a total life of decision.
Christian hope means then, that in Christ, by entrusting
ourselves to him, we can courageously face evil, accept
our own need of further conversion, the lovelessness of
others and the whole legacy of sin in the world around us
and in our own heritage. We can then face death just as
we can face the mammoth task before us which, as St.
Paul explains, is "putting to death our selfish desires."
For this to become possible we need to entrust ourselves
to Christ. We must be determined to assume the senti-
ments of Christ, his own outlook, to walk the path he
paved for us in selfless concern for others.

Let us return once again to the idea so often omitted
in a superficial theology and psychology of hope, to wit,
that judgment is already going on. Those who insist on
selfishly seeking themselves, those who only want to save
their own lives are really wasting their true selves, losing
their lives, spreading frustration and enslaving themselves
more and more to sadness and misery. Judgment is going
on for those who place their trust in themselves, thus
making themselves the center of life instead of Christ,
our hope.

Christ is our saving judgment if we recognize our faults
and if we repent, ready to do penance and to follow him
in hope and courage. The Epistle to the Romans, that
great document of the genuine freedom of the children of
God, sets the direction. The law of the spirit in Christ
has liberated us from the slavery of self-centeredness, of
the collectivity of sinfulness, of the law of sin and solidarity in sinfulness. Christ has freed us from the fear of a

meaningless and hopeless death. "What the law could never do, because our lower nature robbed it of all potency, God has done: by sending his own Son in a form like that of our own sinful nature, so that the commandment of the law may find fulfillment in us, whose conduct, no longer under the control of our lower nature, is directed by the Spirit" (Rom. 8:3–4).

This is the theology of hope so well expressed by St. Paul. He succinctly expressed many ideas in one phrase: our selfish self must be robbed of all its powers, because even with respect to the law of God which is spiritual, good and right, we can maintain a power-seeking attitude and a self-centered, self-protecting outlook. God has manifested the real attitude toward the law, that of redemptive love, by sending his Son in the form of a slave, the One destined to carry the burden of all his brothers in order to demonstrate that selfishness is the way to perdition. As a sacrifice for sin, Christ has passed judgment and therefore man cannot be saved unless he accepts his judgment against sin in a spirit of repentance, sorrow and readiness to make amends.

That Christ is Savior means also that he is the saving conflict with the sinful world, particularly with the self-righteous world of the scribes and Pharisees. He is a saving dissent for all because he protests by his whole life against everything in us which is sinful and niggardly. He does not spare his disciples conflict with those who live on the level of unredeemed man. By his life and by his words, especially by the Paschal Mystery, he teaches us that opposition can be harbinger of hope. For those who know Christ and entrust themselves to him, all the growing pains and polarizations of our age become so many signs and stations of hope.

Hope is not only the greatest gift but also the greatest appeal. In hope, our eyes are opened and our mind is

cleared so that we may see the real commandment of God
as unselfish Christ-like love. Only by entrusting ourselves
to Christ and by accepting him as our rule of conduct,
the model of our life, will our selfish ego be weakened and
our true self become directed by the Spirit who is gift,
anointment in joy and the giver of strength to serve our
brethren.

Christian hope is based on decision and imparts
strength and meaning to our decisions. God has decided
to save us; he has manifested the firm intention to save us,
provided, however, we join in his promise to the world,
receive Christ as his great sign of hope and accept the
Paschal Mystery as the decisive directive. St. Paul continues his hymn of salvation: "Those who live on the level
of our lower nature have their outlook formed by it, and
that spells death; but those who live on the level of the
spirit have the spiritual outlook, and that is life and
peace" (Rom. 8:5–6). The spiritual outlook transforms
our entire being, our desires and decisions in the perspective of the Paschal Mystery, that is, in relation to
Christ, the Messenger of peace and joy who offers himself
as a ransom for all, who entrusts himself to God in the
final prayer on the cross: "Father, into thy hands I commit my spirit." By the power of the Spirit he consecrates
himself for his brethren and thus honors his Father.
Through the gift of the Holy Spirit, the disciples of Christ
receive and gradually assume the outlook of the Pascal
Mystery. St. Paul states quite explicitly that there is no
hope outside of Christ and his spirit: "If a man does not
possess the spirit of Christ he is no Christian" (Rom. 8:9).

Christ is our hope. It follows that hope is not just a
teaching or a catalogue of things to come, but it is Christ
in person. Hope has become incarnate. For Christ's disciples, it means a definite personal relationship. They are
men of hope who have firmly accepted Christ as their

Savior, as their brother and even as their servant. Hope implies a commitment to Christ the Servant, in the service of our brethren. Hope is a new redeeming relationship to Christ with a totally new relationship to all things made in him and to the whole of creation; it is a new relationship with our brothers and sisters in the world around us. This is the existential meaning of a genuine theology of hope and significant catechesis. Both must strive for that clear-sightedness that will lead them to learn from what Christ said, from his life and death, in order to help his disciples learn the power of the gladdening news. Those who are chosen by Christ and who, in turn, have chosen him, our hope, become living witnesses to and instruments of hope in the world.

3
HOPE AS DIALOGUE

Christian hope has a dialogical character in that it can only be explained in terms of interpersonal relationships. God first speaks to us, makes promises and fulfills them, and shares with us his graciousness which the Bible describes as his radiant countenance. This benevolence shines through all his works and deeds. Grace, then, is God's invitation to man for a personal relationship; man is honored and he can communicate joy and peace if he is open to God's gift. This dialogical character entails a responsorial reality, namely, man's awareness and response to God's initiative in gratitude.

God's initiative precedes us in all the events of life. We were first created without being consulted; then throughout our lives we are asked whether or not we want to accept God's design and become ever more to his image and likeness. Our acceptance is indicated by our awareness of the One who created us. We were saved without being asked; again, it is a case of God's initiative in grace; He is the one who first offers us his promises and the pledge of his goodness. Our closeness to Christ, our whole life, can be a response, but we should be fully aware that God's message, God's gift precedes reply. We are open to and receive God's gracious favor if we entrust ourselves to him gratefully.

Hope, then, is always an interpersonal relationship; it is a word that reaches man, a message that moves him, the shalom communicating its peace, but man must be open, attentive, receptive and responsive. Christian hope does not arise from our yearning or desire nor from our option; if our longing for beatitude has vital significance and a saving meaning, it is only because God has so endowed it. In his benevolence, God offers us the fullness of hope in Jesus Christ. Through the Paschal Mystery Christ manifests and awakens hope in us; in our name, he gives the response of trust. This character of hope can never be stressed strongly enough. The initiative is God's own; he first manifests his goodness, kindness, promises, fidelity, and the work he has begun he will fulfill to the day of Christ's second coming.

Hope derives its dynamism from this personal relationship. If you reflect on the most fundamental relationships within the family, you have likely observed the difference between happy children who are loved, loving and trustful and their sad counterparts. Children reflect accurately their parents' attitude toward them. If the parents wanted children, truly desired them and gratefully accepted them from God, such parents realize that they are blessed with their offspring. We then see that the eyes of the little ones and their whole being convey that feeling of hope and trust in their parents. If, however, the children are unwanted, if the parents constantly criticize and punish them, if they take no time to talk with them but maintain a domineering attitude toward them, then we find that the children mirror the parents' behavior in their countenance and their whole being.

Similarly, the phenomenon of scrupulosity can be explained in terms of interpersonal relationships. Any attempt to help a person so afflicted depends upon a true understanding of what it meant for the scrupulous person to have an authoritarian father who dominated fearful children and a frightened mother. The father concept of a policeman in the home has led to a distorted image of God the Father. Research in developmental psychology discloses that we tend to become trustworthy individuals when we are surrounded by trusting and loving persons. If one lives in the midst of hot-tempered people, with malcontent, impatient individuals, his behavior will eventually be affected by such people unless he consciously strives to counteract this influence by a display of kindness, patience and understanding for the people about him.

Hope and despair always imply an interpersonal relationship. In hope, we find two persons interacting and exchanging trust with an increasing readiness to respond to one another's needs. If in this perspective we grasp the notion that by nature man is made for hope and is yearning for beatitude, then we have already received a word of God. It is he who has "spoken out" man in this way; it is his creative word that fashions man for hope. It follows that God never leaves man without hope. It is his creative word, and as Christians, we add that it is God's redemptive word that forever rescues man from sin which, in its fullest sense, is hopelessness. In his innermost being, man is called to hope because God creates so as to have sharers in his beatitude and concelebrants of his triune love. Man is what he is through the One who calls him, so that he may become for others a sign of hope. Thus it is that God calls man in hope for hope and beatitude, but it is a calling in freedom. Man can refuse to become a sign of hope for others; he then declines to become what he should be, what he could be, and he will not come into his own, to that great hope for which he was called.

The whole of God's creation and redemption is a call to hope. Even when man sins, as in the case of Adam and Eve, God does not leave him without hope. There is not one text in the Bible where there is mention of sin and judgment without reference to the hope to which God calls man. Even punishment sent by God is intended as a strong final call for those who did not respond to earlier softer calls to hope. We find that it expresses God's holiness as in the Prophet Hosea: "I will not turn round and destroy you; for I am God and not man, the Holy One in your midst" (Hos. 11:9). God's perfection is God's mercy, and even in punishment he is the healer and is calling to hope. It is of paramount importance in our catechesis and particularly in our pastoral work never to attempt to picture sin alone or to present original sin alone because there exists no such thing in the Bible as a bare treatise on original sin; there is always a summons to hope.

It is God who rescues man from the solidarity of sinfulness and from the slavery of sinfulness, drawing him toward solidarity in hope. Christian hope, in its genuine redeeming sense, implies a firm "yes" to the salvific plan of God. God created us to be sharers and concelebrants of his own beatitude; he manifests this intention finally and fully in Christ. Christ is both the great sacrament of God's promise, of God's calling to hope and of man's response. Christian hope, then, lies in the firm "yes" of trust modeled on our Exemplar, Christ, who at the last moment responded to the Father's calling: "Father, into thy hands I commit my spirit."

It was customary for each Israelite to say every evening: "Into thy hands I commit my spirit." It becomes Christ's testament but he adds one word: "Father." There can be no greater "yes," no greater "amen" to God's prom-

ise, to God's calling to hope than the word of Christ:
"Father, into thy hands I commit my spirit." Even Christ's
last word is preceded by a message of hope for the
brigand on his right: "I tell you this: today you shall be
with me in paradise" (Lk. 23:43). It is his own trust
and the entrusting of himself to the Father that inspires
the final trust, the final hope to all men. St. Paul has
masterfully expressed how Christ's trust in the Father
and in his promises calls us and enables us to be men of
hope. In his second Epistle to the Corinthians, we find:
"The Son of God, Christ Jesus, proclaimed among you by
us, was never a blend of Yes and No. With him it was,
and is, Yes. He is the Yes pronounced upon God's promises, upon every one of them. That is why, when we
give glory to God, it is through Christ Jesus that we say
'Amen'" (2 Cor. 1:19–20).

The above text reminds me of an incident at Vatican
Council II. In our drafting of the *Constitution on the
Church in the Modern World,* we had used the words
"yes" and "amen." One of the conservatives could not
accept this modern language and pleaded with us to
use good old, solid and well-established theological language. We informed him that we had simply adopted
the word of God!

"Yes" and "amen" are basic concepts in the sacred
dialogue recorded in the Bible, and Christ is the "yes."
Indeed, we can say that Christ is the incarnation of God's
"yes" to man and that after all our failures, all our sins,
God's covenant remains firm. Christ is confirmed and
anointed by the Spirit to be the fullest testimony of trust
and hope. He is the embodiment of God's salvific will
and of God's saving presence. He is at the same time
God's promise and man's hope through his full acceptance in our name. He is the Covenant, as the ancient
Fathers of the Church used to say; in him there is full

representation for he stands for all. He makes visible in his own trust and in the way he entrusts himself to the Father that mankind can trust in God's merciful fidelity. Christ is the "amen" and he utters it throughout his life. His life blood seals the "yes" of absolute trust and hope. He is the full visibility of God's undeserved grace and graciousness. In him the Father turns his countenance to us. He makes his design of hope fully manifest in the One who is the visible image of the invisible God. Christ is the explicit and attractive image of God's salvific love.

The character of hope arising from grace is a sign of the undeserved graciousness of God calling man to acknowledge, without any security-insecurity complexes and without anguish, that he is surely unable by himself to promote peace and trust or repair the damage wrought by sin. But man can entrust himself to God in all his weakness, in all his sinfulness and with all his failures. This is a part of Christian hope. Such hope is not a mysticism of sin that allows man to say: "I can continue to sin because of the salvific plan of God to rescue man." On the contrary—hope likens him to Christ; it awakens and frees all his energies for good. The starting point, the great perspective, is one of grateful acceptance of the undeserved gift and the subsequent entrusting of oneself to God's graciousness.

Faith, hope and love all have this dialogical character. Where the responsorial aspect does not come through, we find that man is still prisoner of his own ego. It is especially in prayer that man comes to the fullest awareness of this dialogical reality, to the fullest consciousness that it is God's own word that enables us to respond. God first speaks to us; man listens, opens himself, treasures up the words and dwells in the Word. But there is no possibility of abiding in the Word or of letting the Word dwell in us unless we are ready to give the full response, that of sharing the Word and sharing our joy as instruments of hope. Before God, man assumes an ever greater responsorial character in the full sense of the words: response, responsibility and co-responsibility.

Emphasis on the dialogical character of hope has inevitable consequences, for instance, as to the grouping of the eschatological virtues which provide the full orchestration to hope. Leading all others should be gratitude. The origin of hope does not lie in man's futurology or any kind of utopia but in what God has already done for us. His promises come to us with his deeds, his gifts to humanity and to each individual. Gratitude should also be included for all that is worthwhile in tradition, that investment of goodness, wisdom and justice in response to God's gifts and in co-operation with him.

It is precisely at this point that my vision of hope differs in emphasis and approach from Jürgen Moltmann's theology of hope. He stresses the futurology of man and gives full attention to an open future. There is no doubt that hope looks forward to an ever greater future and to all that God's loving providence holds in store for us, but our expectations must be based on gratitude and thanksgiving for the very origin of hope. The guarantor of the open future is God himself, his presence and all that he has already revealed and wrought in creation.

Undue emphasis on the future, especially when tinged with a somewhat utopian and scientific futurology could well promote a new kind of Pelagianism and entail a loss of continuity with respect to the vision of salvation history. When man fashions his own dreams about the future and sets out to take the future into his own hands, he is endangering that future. He will tend to pay too little attention to God's word and work as revealed in the ongoing history of salvation.

I am not intimating that hope should not give rise to

healthy speculation and imagination about the future. On the contrary, the dynamic character of our age demands strong emphasis on an "open" future, but in trusting praise of God who has done great things and who promises to accomplish unprecedented new wonders. The good steward will always seek a happy balance between the *nova et vetera*. Grateful regard for the past can be linked to the here-and-now with its inherent dynamism toward the future. This will ensure that vital, wholesome equilibrium between continuity of life and the courage to take risks.

4
HOPE AS SOLIDARITY IN LOVE

If egotism spells a hopeless existence in the deleterious companionship of sinners, hope initiates liberation in solidarity looking toward the unity of all men. Hope in solidarity means unity in genuine love.

During the early centuries of our era, Christ was often referred to as the Covenant. In him, the Father offers his alliance to mankind and to creation. Christ, the radical embodiment of solidarity, offers himself in the name of all men; the blood of the Redeemer becomes the law of solidarity since it stands for all. It is thus the "blood of the new and everlasting covenant" offered for all. Christ is the sacrament of solidarity who confirms historically that salvation is wrought in solidarity with him, the Incarnate Word of God; he unites all men in his all-embracing sacrificial love. He did not come to redeem isolated, separated souls; he came to redeem man in his wholeness: body, soul and spirit, personal and communitarian man, man *per se* and the man of worldly realities.

A fully functioning person is never self-sufficient; self-realization comes from "being with" the source of all personhood in heaven and on earth. Such is the reality God has revealed to us about his own personal life; the Father exists by "being with" his Son, by expressing himself in the Word, and the Holy Spirit is the Father's being with the Son in love. It follows that the human person created in the image and likeness of the Triune God cannot be an isolated being; man is a gift "spoken out" by God's love. In creating man to be a concelebrant of his love, God inserts him in a human family, prototype of all social life, for it is only in community that one finds trust and love. Man can only respond to his calling by living in responsibility and co-responsibility.

The human person comes to gradual self-realization through and for the community by sharing all his personal assets and abilities in common with others. Personality growth comes from the sharing of human experiences, reflections, co-reflections and traditions while retaining the capacity to reshape them for the common good. A person lives in co-responsibility when, together with others, he responds to Christ's rallying call. We come to our true selves, to our genuine individuality and unique name when we respond to Christ who calls us together and invites us to open ourselves in love to our brothers and sisters. Co-responsibility in the here-and-now comprises a sense of gratitude for the generations that have accumulated wisdom and a wealth of insights, experiences and reflections out of responsibility for future generations.

The world in which we live has inherited an accumulation of wrongdoing, selfishness and oppressive power structures. This investment of sinfulness reflected in the culture, traditions and collective prejudices constitutes a constant source of temptation. However, as believers we realize even more that grateful acknowledgment must be given to God's wisdom, goodness and justice evident in today's culture and handed down to us by the countless

righteous people who have shared experiences and co-reflections in their common striving for holiness through
thousands of years. Thus we can also realistically accept
the fact that our legacy of strengths and good deeds from
generations past is weighted down by a weakened heritage and a sinful environment.

Sin was first introduced in the world when man failed
to respond fully to God's initial plan. God, the Creator,
fashioned us for oneness and for solidarity; man was
meant to share in co-responsibility. The Book of Genesis
is more than a mere chronicle; it reveals God's original
design: man and woman are made for each other; they
are equally created in the image and likeness of God and
are joined together in the presence of God in mutual
gratitude. Their joint acceptance in the presence of the
Creator prefigures the whole of mankind. Then sin comes
along; Eve, alone with the serpent of her selfishness, desires personal freedom, greater wisdom and more power.
The great theological vision of the sacred author speaks
of an interruption of communion with God, that is, the
discontinuance of adoration, of dialogue with God. Instead, Eve initiates a monologue, pursues her selfish interests and unavoidably leads to Adam's contamination
with the ensuing solidarity in sinfulness which tradition
calls "original sin."

The breakdown of genuine solidarity gives rise to solidarity in evil. Original sin, then, started chronologically
with one who could have done good but did not, who
could have avoided evil but did not. However, it is not
the case of a single couple burdening the whole human
race with a bad heritage. We are all Adam and Eve; we
invest in selfishness when we fail to do the good we are
called to do, when we refuse to invest goodness, kindness
and gentleness in human history. The author of Genesis
makes it clear that Adam and Eve were not solely respon-

sible for the evil that besets man; agreed, they indulged in futile pursuits but their descendant Cain indulged in much greater sinfulness. Cain was not, chronologically, the first son of Adam for he could not have been a city builder. He is son in the broad sense of being a descendant, but he represents those in whom sinfulness has come to a peak.

In Genesis again, there is mention of Lamech as the fourth descendant of Cain; sin has greatly multiplied in him. Lamech, a domineering polygamist, threatens his wives: "Wives of Lamech, mark what I say: I kill a man for wounding me, a young man for a blow. Cain may be avenged seven times, but Lamech seventy-seven" (Gen. 4:23-24). This is a biblical indication of how sin can perpetuate itself, but this need not necessarily be so. The family of Abel is replaced by Seth where once again man began to adore God; sin is overcome at least to some extent.

So original sin is not just handed on by procreation as St. Augustine thought, nor is it a stain on the soul that can simply be washed away by baptism as stated in the Baltimore catechism; original sin relates to the tremendous mystery of solidarity. God has made man for solidarity because he is the one Creator; his whole creative work manifests oneness, solidarity. However, man is called to unity in freedom; man remains free either to accept or refuse solidarity in good. Should he refuse, he falls into the solidarity of evil where the powers of selfishness, individualism and group-egotism prevail; in short, he joins the company of domineering egotists.

The life of Joseph Stalin illustrates the point. As a seminarian, Stalin formed a Marxist ring. The fact was brought to the attention of the seminary authorities who soon dismissed him. Stalin immediately gave the director the names of all the students who held membership in the

Marxist circle. Later, in the course of his differences with Trotzky, someone reminded him that he had proved himself a traitor from the very beginning, to which he replied: "You are an idiot from beginning to end. If I had not given that list to the director, these cowards would have become coward priests. I forced them to stand together." This is solidarity in evil.

Stalin later organized the Communist party in Georgia, in the southern part of Russia. He did not seek support for his organization from the poor; he collected money from the most wealthy people, telling them quite bluntly: "You are paying for the Communist party" and each one was told how much he had to contribute. When anybody refused, Stalin served notice that he and his men would return in two weeks at which time double the amount would have to be paid. Most people paid at once; those who did not, suffered property damage from fire and explosions so that restoration and repairs were even more costly. When Stalin and his friends returned, they received payment in full.

Stalin was once caught on the spot by the Czarist police while extorting payment from a capitalist. The officer said: "Now we have proof." "Oh no," said Stalin, "it was my friend who forced me to accept this money." The intimidated capitalist then rescued Stalin by confirming his statement: "I forced him to accept the money." The capitalist, very concerned about his material possessions, did not want to be burned out. Thus capitalists were truly financing their own destruction. In my opinion this historical incident illustrates magnificently the mystery of original sin, the accumulated power of individualism and self-centeredness; the more such power is amassed, the stronger the ties become. Finally, the situation is nothing other than a veritable hell, with selfish people living in the full solidarity of evil with other selfish people.

We must always remember, however, that it is not just Adam and Eve who got the sin ball rolling, but all of us who fail to live in genuine co-responsibility with each other. Happily, God has never left man without hope. There is Abel contributing goodness, offering a sacrifice of trust. There is the genealogy of those who by serving God evince the presence of God in man. Even Cain is marked by the sign of God's protection so that a total self-destruction of sinners is avoided.

Finally, salvation becomes fully manifest in Christ who bears the burden of man. The tremendous sacramentality of solidarity in Christ's death is already forecast and partially revealed at the baptism of Jesus in the Jordan by John the Baptist. The ritual baptism of repentance was a very existential, prophetic anticipation of the baptism on the cross, the baptism in the blood of the Redeemer. Christ wanted to be baptized during the general baptism (Lk. 3:21) where the "bad characters" came to John the Baptist to be cleansed in repentance. Christ thus indicated that his baptism meant the liberation of all through the One who bears the burdens of others, the sins of his brethren. He intended that they also bear the burdens of one another (Gal. 6:2). It is more than symbolic that Jesus was crucified surrounded by brigands and that he responded to the one who had come to appreciate saving solidarity with him: "I tell you this, today you shall be with me in paradise" (Lk. 23:43). Christ is the embodiment, the incarnation of redeeming solidarity not only in the ritual celebration of baptism in the Jordan but throughout his life and death. In terms of human history, it implies that each of us is called to make a choice as to whether he wants to associate himself with Christ in saving solidarity and hope or remain within the clutches of sinful, pernicious solidarity. There is no way out of original sin save by accepting existentially and wholeheart-

edly solidarity in Christ. Only then does baptism become
the sign of salvation, the sacrament of hope in solidarity.

In this perspective are we to understand the biblical
texts bearing on solidarity. In his Epistle to the Ephesians,
Paul writes: "I entreat you as a prisoner for the Lord's
sake. As God has called you, live up to your calling. Be
humble always and gentle and patient too. Be forbearing
with one another and charitable. Spare no effort to make
fast with bonds of peace the unity which the Spirit gives"
(Eph. 4:1–16). At the very heart of the theology of hope
is the Holy Spirit in whom and through whom Christ is
sent to the poor and is anointed to dedicate himself for
all. The mission of the Spirit through the risen Lord is a
calling to spare no effort of hope in solidarity. "There is
one body, one Spirit as there is also one hope held out in
God's call to you" (Eph. 4:4). Here we see the great theological vision of Paul, the prisoner of Christ, totally given
to the saving mystery of Christ in solidarity with all men
and the whole of creation, calling everybody and everything to hope through this solidarity.

Paul is entreating the disciples of Christ to make fast
with bonds of peace the unity which is the gift of the
Holy Spirit. The Spirit himself is the bond of peace, the
bond of unity in saving solidarity. "There is one body and
one spirit as there is one hope." The body of Christ who
is anointed by the one Spirit is the body given for all.
Christ, the Anointed, gives his body and blood "for the
life of the world" (Jn. 6:51). In the eucharist, Christ unceasingly gives himself for the life of the world, and those
who receive him, not only physically but in faith and
hope by the grace of the Spirit, will give themselves for
the life of the world in the power of the same Holy Spirit.

The fourth chapter of the Epistle to the Ephesians is
permeated with hope: "There is one hope held out for you
in God's call to you" (Eph. 4:4). Salvation truth and bap-

tism remind us that there is no hope for the isolationist, the individualist or the egotist. One who seeks only to save his soul while remaining unconcerned about the world is, by necessity, lost because he remains ensnared in sinful solidarity. He loses his soul because there is only one hope, which is solidarity with Christ.

The Church Fathers spoke of Christ as the rallying call. The catechism of the Council of Trent says: *Ecclesia, id est convocatio,* the Church is the rallying call in Christ; we are called to hope in togetherness. St. Paul continues: "One Lord, one faith, one baptism; one God and Father of all, who is over all and through all and in all. But each of us has been given his gift, his due portion of Christ's bounty" (Eph. 4:5-7). Each one of us has received his own individual gifts, but all in view of the saving solidarity by the one Spirit, for the one Body of Christ, to the glory of the one Lord and through the one baptism in the Spirit. This central truth of salvation obliges us to use our gifts in the service of all; otherwise, they are lost. Salvation in hope cannot tolerate motives directed fundamentally toward self-fulfillment; hope is a matter of consecration, dedication and giving of oneself. God will then take care of our personal fulfillment. If we seek primarily self-enhancement in self-determination, then the powers of evil will take over and keep us in the deleterious solidarity of sin.

Paul then emphasizes the variety of God's gifts but always with a view to solidarity. "And these were his gifts: some to be apostles, some prophets, some evangelists, some pastors and teachers, to equip God's people for work in his service, to the building up of the body of Christ. So shall we all at last attain to the unity inherent in our faith and our knowledge of the Son of God—to mature manhood, measured by nothing less than the full stature of Christ" (Eph. 4:11-13). All charisms and ministries are

46 HOPE IS THE REMEDY

signs of hope for all, if received and used in saving solidarity. "Let us speak the truth in love; so shall we fully grow up into Christ. He is the head and on him the whole body depends. Bonded and knit together by every constituent joint, the whole frame grows through the due activity of each part, and builds itself up in love" (Eph. 4: 15–16). This chapter of Ephesians has a magnificent leitmotiv and program of hope in solidarity as well as solidarity in hope; there can be no hope without saving solidarity.

The Pastoral Constitution on the Church in the Modern World (*Gaudium et spes*), drafted by Vatican Council II, emphasizes Christian personalism in all its dimensions of community and solidarity as suggested by the Pauline text. The Council Fathers expressed their conviction that a person is not a being existing for himself. The human person finds his true self through consecration for others, by being with and for one's neighbor in the service of the common good. Articles 11 and 12 very strongly emphasize the whole vision of the Church as the body of Christ, the community of love in solidarity. In Article 24, there is a classical formulation which can be summarized as man's being unable to truly find himself except through a sincere gift of himself. The following article states: "When the structure of affairs is flawed by the consequences of sin, man, already born with a bent toward evil, finds there new inducements to sin, which cannot be overcome without strenuous efforts and the assistance of grace" (*Gaudium et spes*, Art. 25). A later article refers to solidarity as a sign of the kingdom of God: "Whoever in obedience to Christ seeks first the kingdom of God will as a consequence receive a stronger and purer love for helping all his brothers and for perfecting the work of justice under the inspiration of charity" (*Gaudium et spes*, Art. 72).

The defeat of individualism turned out to be one of the most important achievements of Vatican II. From beginning to end, in every decree and document, we sense that kind of personalism which means a "yes" to community, a being with, a commitment to and a freedom in the sense that one is liberated from selfishness to be consecrated by the Spirit for the service of all. The Spirit makes us the body of Christ who gives his body for the life of the world.

It is very important that in prayer, in our personal motivation, in theological study and in catechetical work we return again and again to this vision of Christ, one of absolute solidarity with all of mankind, with the whole of creation. He is the Savior of the world in his body and blood; he calls to the new heaven and the new earth in solidarity. He is the saving sign of hope as the all-embracing sacrament of solidarity. He wants us to be witnesses of this hope in solidarity, visibly and effectively, and through us, his disciples, he wants others to be consecrated to the same work.

5

FAITH FOUNDED ON HOPE

Hope tests the mettle of our faith. A proper understanding of this truth will help us grasp the interrelatedness of faith, hope and love in proper perspective.

Hope is faith and love on pilgrimage; it is not something apart from faith or love. Hope is the internal dynamism of faith and love, a concept poorly understood by a rationalistic and all too Hellenistic approach to faith. When faith is approached by reason alone, it is presented as a system of well-defined truths, a catalogue of beliefs in an Establishment theology strongly influenced by canon law. Of course, there are abiding truths, it cannot be denied, but only in the One and through the One who is the fullness of truth. Our human concepts are never the full truth; they are tainted by the pilgrim situation of the thinker.

The biblical concept of faith refers to trust in the Lord, the faithful One, who pledged to remain with mankind and so gradually to reveal himself to us. Salvific faith consists in entrusting oneself to the One who reveals himself as the Way, the Truth and the Life. It is trust in the Lord of history, in him who was, is and will come, who is present in his work and in ongoing creation. Faith can thus be described in relation to salvation history of which we are a part; it is a reality in which we are involved with God. In faith, the heart of the matter lies in the history of God with man in his world and the history of men with God in openness to God's revealing action.

According to dogmatic theology, revelation came to an end with the death of the last Apostle or with Christ, but this truth should not be misunderstood. Christ is truly the final Word; God will never send any greater word, message, comfort or truth to the world than Christ because he is the Word Incarnate. He is the fullness of revelation, the center of revelation. But Christ is still on the way toward his final coming. He has revealed himself once in his incarnation, life, death and resurrection but only in view of his final coming in the Parousia. So revelation in Christ's life some 1970 years ago does not bring history to an end but opens up new horizons for history, because Christ continues his work and manifests his design in an ongoing revelation. To the very end of history, man must pay attention to Christ's word if he is to come to an understanding of God's salvific plan: "My Father has never ceased his work, and I am working too" (Jn. 5:17). God's work is always enlightening and his words are trust-inspiring because they constitute a progressive unveiling of the total plan of God.

There is a very striking vision in the fifth chapter of the Book of Revelation about the Book of History sealed with seven seals. The question arises in heaven: Who can unseal the Book? There is silence and expectation followed by a liberating response: the Lamb who stands before the throne of God, "the Lion from the tribe of Judah, the Root of David has won the right to open the scroll and break its seven seals" (Rev. 5:5). The Book is then unsealed but interestingly enough, nobody reads. There are events, the

great happenings of history, but understood in the light
of Christ, understood as preparing his final coming; there
are new events and thus a continuing message. So all of
history is an ongoing revelation; it is not something apart
from Christ nor is it something in the sense of those who
speak of a post-Christian era when things are better understood without Christ. That amounts to a denial of
faith. It is in Christ, in view of Christ, through the gift of
Christ, through the gift of the Holy Spirit, in the community of the faithful looking to Christ that history can be understood as a continuous revelation. The great Actor is
the Word in whom all things were made and who has
come to redeem history. Therefore, every event is also a
word of the Word.

In the Hebrew language the word *dabar* means both
event and word, so that all the events of history, all the
signs of revelation are a word, a message, a disclosure. All
things are made in the Word, and there is not one thing
that is not made in him; he is the Word. Therefore, historical events have a character of revelation about them for
those who look to Christ, for those who, through the Spirit
of Christ, are open-minded. For a Christian to become
complacent to the point of asserting that he has known
everything for a long time or that he knows all the answers would mean total unfaithfulness to God disclosing
his majesty, wisdom and salvific designs in the events and
ongoing endeavors of the community of believers. All
events are to be seen in the light of Christ.

Salvation history and all of human history as such, past
and present, are to be seen as an integral part of the
Christian faith. Faith in Christ makes human history infinitely more interesting and more dynamic than philosophical systems because it constantly manifests new
horizons and introduces new perspectives. Therefore,
faith calls for total openness to events, to all that God

does and wills to do in human history; faith also summons us to trust in the Lord of history. Such openness comprises praise for all the marvelous deeds performed and for the unique fact that he has revealed himself in his servant and Son, Jesus Christ. Faith thus becomes a constant doxology or praise of God with the realization that events are encounters with a God infinitely greater than anything our words, concepts or theology can ever express. Through hope the believer finds himself trustfully on the way with the God of history, looking forward to his constant coming.

The dynamics of faith prompt us toward a better knowledge of God in ever greater love and trust. This hope characteristic of faith is very evident in the Epistle to the Hebrews: "And what is faith? Faith gives substance to our hopes, and makes us certain of realities we do not see" (Heb. 11:1). Faith is essentially dynamic in character; it is based on hope. Faith gives assurance to our hopes because God does not reveal abstract philosophical ideas but trust-inspiring truths of salvation. In every age, he points the way leading to salvation.

"It is for their faith that men of old stand on record" (Heb. 11:2). Paul then indicates how hope motivated the faith of the patriarchs and many other people who belonged to Israel and others who did not; these people evince faith in their openness to new events. "By faith, Abraham obeyed the call to go out to a land destined for himself and his heirs, and left home without knowing where he was to go" (Heb. 11:8). "By faith, Abraham, when the test came, offered up Isaac . . . for he reckoned that God had power even to raise from the dead" (Heb. 11:17–19). "By faith, Moses left Egypt, and not because he feared the king's anger; for he was resolute, as one who saw the invisible God" (Heb. 11:27).

Hope characterizes Isaac's blessing and the whole life

of Joseph. "By faith, Isaac blessed Jacob and Esau and spoke of things to come. By faith Joseph, at the end of his life, spoke of the departure of Israel from Egypt, and instructed them what to do with his bones" (Heb. 11: 20–22). It is ironic that some religious congregations and theological schools pay more attention to the dead bones of their founders than to their spirit. They have forgotten the first part of Joseph's instructions, namely, the "departure," and so failed to see the challenge of hope in the "bones." It is worth noting that not even dead bones should remain in the same place; even the bones should "depart."

"By faith Moses, when he grew up, refused to be called the son of Pharaoh's daughter, preferring to suffer hardship with the people of God rather than enjoy the transient pleasures of sin. He considered the stigma that rests on God's Anointed greater wealth than the treasures of Egypt" (Heb. 11:24–27). This text particularly stresses the idea that salvific faith frees from every kind of security complex. It is obvious that in all the aforementioned persons Paul finds the same vision of faith as dynamic, as a readiness to look forward and to confront the novelty of trying experiences with trust in the Lord of history. Through hope, faith is more closely related to events than to any set of formulated truths.

"And what of ourselves? With all these witnesses to faith around us like a cloud, we must throw off every encumbrance, every sin to which we cling, and run with resolution the race for which we are entered, our eyes fixed on Jesus, on whom faith depends from start to finish" (Heb. 12:1–2). So it is a setting out, as Paul insists, the running of a race, looking to what is ahead and forgetting what is behind (Phil. 3:12–14). Evidently, faith cannot be imprisoned in an Establishment; the point must be made very clear to those persons whose "faith" is shaken because their well-memorized answers from the Baltimore catechism are no longer pertinent. Like a venerable grandfather in old age, they are people who like to keep repeating stories of their younger days, thinking they will be of interest to today's youth. Theirs is truly an Establishment concept of faith. However, concepts and words derive their connotation from the historical context, and when they turn up in a different period of history, they change their meaning. But because of its relationship to hope, faith is much more than a well-defined set of fully explained concepts. Faith is a call of the Lord of history and a response of man to the challenging events of the history of salvation in the ongoing history of man and God. Therefore we should not be shocked to find that only gradually do we come to a better appreciation of faith in its existential character; salvific faith is a trustful encounter with the God of history. Faith means one is on the road with him. It is particularly in times of trial, in periods of transition and profound change, that God summons to greater trust, calls for a more radical entrusting of ourselves to him and for a more painstaking effort to understand the signs of the times.

Christian faith is quite different from any kind of ideology, philosophy or closed system of thought. It is a daring earthly history of man with God, leading toward the fullness of light and life. It is through the intrinsic dynamism of hope that faith directs us simultaneously to the here-and-now and toward the final fulfillment. Faith is life, a trustful life in the light of Jesus, but nevertheless in partial darkness because it is an encounter with a mystery which is always infinitely greater than anything man can grasp in his earthly life. St. Paul expressed the idea well in his first letter to the Corinthians: "Now we see only puzzling reflections in a mirror, but then we shall see face to face" (1 Cor. 13:12). We must try to understand this thought more thoroughly; what we see, what our words express, what the catechism teaches us, what theologians say: all these things taken together are but a puzzling reflection. Woe to us if we feel we "possess" the truth totally and refuse to exert new efforts, for without constant openness and an unrelenting, trustful attempt to grasp past events in the light of the here-and-now with a view to the future, we have denied the mystery of faith. Faith never allows complacency, establishment or a lazy repetition of formulas. Repeated indefinitely, earlier formulations fail to be the message of the living God of history. There must be a constant effort to appropriate God's words, to understand them more deeply in the context of ongoing events which are disclosures of his salvific plan and loving design for us.

Faith can attain a profound firmness through unflagging hope and trust in the Lord of history, but with respect to the expression of the mystery of God and of his design, our faith is always infinitely imperfect. St. Thomas Aquinas explains this concept by analogy, as similitude in ever greater dissimilitude. What we see and are able to express now has a certain similarity with the event we hope for in the final fulfillment, but we should remember that this holds true because of the ever greater dissimilitude of all our knowledge and achievements in comparison with God's total design. Faith filled with hope is truly the way manifesting the right direction if we join the pilgrim Church in her definitions, her guidelines and her preaching of the Gospel, but faith is only a directive, a similitude pointing in the right direction. It must not be confused with truth as dwelling in God nor with that splendor which will be made manifest at the day of fulfillment. Faith includes a constant call for growth, for greater depth, for clearer vision and for a broader perspective in total awareness of our limitations.

This viewpoint was thoroughly discussed at Vatican Council II when the theologians of the Holy Office presented their draft on the two sources of revelation, namely, the Bible and tradition. For them, tradition seemed to be a kind of library containing specifically those books recording all the decisions of the Holy Office and other curial bodies. They were thoroughly mistaken in viewing faith almost as if it were a catalogue of beliefs, a frozen tradition, an Establishment. Faith confronts us with the torrent of life. Tradition means a continuity of life with God keeping things going, keeping us alive, opening our eyes, arousing us from time to time, assisting the Church in her direction but not allowing her any self-complacency or indulgence in formalism. Tradition is a torrent of life; it is alive because of the presence of the living God in the ongoing history of salvation. Faith in Israel and in the Church of Christ is kept alive by the great prophets who shake the Establishment when there is danger of the Church's falling into ritualism and formalism.

In the history of salvation, we find discontinuity because of our sins and a totally different but salvific discontinuity when God sends prophets, great saints like Pope John, telling us very clearly that we can not settle down, that we have to try to grasp the vital meaning of the here-and-now in the light of total tradition and in responsibility for the future. There are, then, two different discontinuities; one is based on our sins and the other is a discontinuity caused by God, ever faithful, who mercifully opens our eyes and gives us a new chance for a deeper conversion. It is very important that our concept of tradition be a right one, that it allow us to set out courageously on the saving way to the future but with trust in the living God. He remains faithful to himself while gradually manifesting new things which disclose his master design in absolute fidelity to it.

Again, the community of faith must never err by confining itself to a bare exploration of the Bible. The priests and Pharisees, scribes and lawyers—theologians and canonists of Israel—all explored the Bible, endeavoring to explain each text and discuss each word, but they were not open to the signs of the times, to the great presence of God in his servant and Son, Jesus Christ. They concentrated on dead texts, looking only to the written word and to lifeless formulas.

The Church, the bride of Christ, should be recognized by her openness to the signs of the times. The Council calls "signs of the times" those cues to the salvific presence of God. For believers, all events, particularly those concerning the unity and brotherhood of man, are a call to openness. The Church as a community of faith is on pilgrimage with the Lord of history, but she will never lose heart when confronted with new events and problems because she always walks with the same Lord Jesus Christ. Our epoch must become more Christian, more Christ-like, that is, more aware of the fidelity of Christ to himself in new events, aware that he is urging all of us to live in today's context according to his love disclosed once and forever. He reveals himself in his covenant with man in history and throughout history with a view to his final coming. Faith, then, consists essentially in these two aspects: a grateful "yes" to what God has already done and manifested, but also a trustful openness and expectancy toward what he will do and reveal, and vigilance for what he actually calls for here and now. Christian faith is an encounter of the total human person with the Lord of history revealing himself and his design about history. It is only through trust and hope that the believer remains in salvific contact with the history of salvation.

When God reveals himself in his events through his Word that is acting and creative, he calls for a spontaneous response. Faith therefore means also that we be ready to act on the word. I chose the title *Acting on the Word* for my book about the evangelical counsels because of the centrality of his theme in the Sermon on the Mount. Christ, after revealing his salvific plan in the new law of the beatitudes, insists: "'Not everyone who calls me "Lord, Lord" will enter the kingdom of Heaven, but only those who do the will of my heavenly Father'" (Mt. 7:21). "'What then of the man who hears these words of mine and acts upon them? He is like a man who had the sense to build his house on rock. The rain came down, the floods rose, the wind blew, and beat upon the house; but it did not fall, because its foundations were on rock. But what of the man who hears these words of mine and does not act upon them? He is like a man who was foolish enough to build his house on sand. The rain came down, the floods rose, the wind blew, and beat upon that house; down it fell with a great crash.' When Jesus had finished this discourse the people were astounded at his teaching; unlike their own teachers he taught with a note of authority" (Mt. 7:24–29). Behind the spoken word of historical events, there is the great Event, the Creator, the Word, the Redeemer. Faith cannot be separated from a readiness to act upon the word according to present opportunities.

Whenever faith is accepted merely as a closed system of well-defined dogmas or formulations, dogma itself is misunderstood and such a faith loses its dynamic structure of hope and loses contact with the living God. Salvific faith is a surrender to God, who reveals himself and discloses his salvific intentions by acting, by a dynamic word, by an ongoing series of events and by the dynamism of his gracious gifts. Therefore to say "yes" in faith and hope already implies a willingness to act accordingly. Faith never achieves fullness; it remains a hopeful beginning, a constant setting out, an ever-renewed readiness to receive the word and act upon it. Faith thus bears the future in itself. For the believer, the future has already begun. Faith is filled with the divine promises and with the dynamic presence of salvation history that never allows us to settle down. Faith points in a clear direction to an open horizon, thus investing both the past and the present with the fecundity of his promises.

6
THE DYNAMISM OF HOPE:
FAITH ACTIVE IN LOVE

Hope is the dynamic force of growing faith and love. Hope or faith or love cannot be looked upon as being separate from each other; they are alive and true to the extent that they form a synthesis. Faith is God's gift to man by which he attains man's innermost being, revealing himself in love toward all men and toward the whole of creation. Through the believer, God expects to receive a response of gratitude and true love. It is through God's grace in faith that man opens himself to God's self-revealing love, responding to God's design to be a sharer and a concelebrant of his love.

Faith entails a sincere openness to divine truth, to all of God's salvific revelation. The Bible is not free from glaring imperfections and scientific errors, because God never intended to reveal biology and astronomy by miracles. Knowledge in the natural and physical sciences has to be acquired painstakingly; however, it is the Creator himself who gives us the power, energy and intelligence to discover the marvels of creation. But this unfolding knowledge does not constitute revelation of God's salvific plan with which faith alone is concerned. The Bible and all of God's revelation is free from error when directing man on the path toward salvation through an ever deeper knowledge and understanding of God's love. Now as ever, God wants to share his love as fully as possible as man wends his way on pilgrimage toward a perfect sharing in the beatific vision.

We may well ask: Will man ever realize God's salvific plan? If man does what God told him to do, he will come to realize more fully that everything comes from God; he will constantly grow in love and in appreciation of God's benevolence. When faith is severed from love, it becomes a dead faith. Here lie the dangers and pitfalls of a theology and catechesis that defined faith mainly as an intellectual assent to a set of dogmas and formulas with little regard for its vital confrontation with God who is love and for its bearing fruit in love. Without the dynamism of love and hope, faith is dead. To speak of faith without love and hope is comparable to defining man without life, as a corpse, a dead body already in a state of putrefaction. Who would dare say that this is man? By a miracle God can raise to life a faith that is merely intellectual or content to toy with formulas, but it is a miracle as great as the resurrection of a dead body.

Faith is really defined as a response in love, an initial and growing response to God revealing himself, his love and his design to man so as to lead him toward the final and full concelebration of his love. Therefore, it implies a faith that is alive, marked by hope and growth, openness and love. Faith is an initial response in love to bear fruit in love, united to God's love for man and creation. However, man's response is truthful to the extent that he remains constantly open and disposed to grow in hope of final fulfillment.

During the Counter Reformation theologians reacted against the one-sided Protestant definition of faith which held the assurance that God would be "my" Savior; the believer had found a merciful Savior for himself. The *fides fiducialis* reducing faith to one's own personal salvation was a vague and very individualistic understanding of faith. Catholic theologians responded by trying to explain faith as a "yes" to an objective truth, as something capable of guaranteeing a community of faith. Since the apostolic era, Christians have shared a common creed; it is very important for the pilgrim Church to maintain this bond. But we share in salvation truth only when faith unites us in readiness to act on the word and to entrust ourselves to the Lord of history in a common effort to decipher the signs of the times.

It behooves us to rid ourselves of that narrow definition of faith as mere intellectual assent; it is imperative that we relate it to hope and to the dynamic revelation of God's loving call for response in love to his readiness to share his love with all men. Faith, hope and love together constitute the one great reality that can make man responsive to the ongoing manifestation of God's salvific plan. A life of faith, hope and love constitutes the great reality between the first and the second coming of Christ by which God prepares us for the final event in history.

Without the dynamism of an ever greater love and hope, and unless hope impels us to work for a better knowledge of God and of man, faith becomes a stinking corpse. St. James is even more drastic in his expression: "You have faith enough to believe that there is one God. Excellent! The devils have faith like that, and it makes them tremble" (Jas. 2:19). That kind of intellectual faith divorced from the dynamism of hope and love is hell; the man of barren "faith" is condemned to sterility. However, in all humility, we must realize that the faith of the pilgrim community of faith is never sufficiently consummate in love. Faith needs the structure of hope, that con-

stant yearning to know and love God better, to respond
with greater docility to his invitation, his calling and the
manifestation of his loving design so as to serve him better.

The foundation of faith and hope lies in the creative
and redemptive presence of the love of God. God lovingly
reveals himself in the Covenant and restores his people
through repentance, forgiveness and reconciliation to a
deeper understanding of the covenant and a more faithful
witness to the world. Growth in faith means a constant
openness to the love of God as God reveals himself in
the context of history and in the concrete situations of
daily life. I think that this vision of faith, which is certainly biblical and which was strongly emphasized at
Vatican Council II and recorded in the official conciliar
documents, can and should preserve us from a noxious
security complex to which we are prone. We can entrust
ourselves totally to God and render a sincere obedience of
faith out of responsibility for the world, even if we harbor
doubt about some doctrines that have little or no significance for our relationship to God and for brotherhood in
Christ.

How little we know about so many things and how
much more we would like to know! But I dare to ask: Do
we not really have greater assurance today because of a
more vital vision of faith, hope and love? I think there is
greater certainty about the essentials today because we
have come to a better understanding of the event of faith
as a calling to a total commitment to God and his plan. In
this commitment we will not be shaken if there emerge,
for example, different definitions of original sin or different
theories about natural law, provided the focal point of
faith becomes more alive for us. Even today's uncertain-
ties that cause us to suffer can be signs of hope when we
entrust ourselves to an ever-loving God with keener
awareness that God is and always remains infinitely

greater than any of our concepts about him. When certainties relative to matters irrelevant to our salvific life have been discarded, the essential truths constitute a stronger urge to entrust ourselves more fully to God in our constant search for ways of responding to him in the totality of our lives. Faith then acquires greater depth and attains greater firmness and fecundity.

Hope is faith and love in this in-between time. In faith we have joyously and gratefully received the One who is the Truth, the Way, the Life, and we are now living our grateful response by entrusting ourselves to him; we are thus on pilgrimage with him in the community of faith and hope, ready to greet him when he comes in the guise of current events, and we joyously await his final coming. The love we have already experienced in faith and the way God has already manifested his love draw our attention and our hopes to that love as yet unseen but promised. This vision of hope, faith and love imparts a definite orientation to Christian morality.

When viewed in an existential way, the Creed points to our constant commitment to the glory of God in loving solidarity. *We* believe in one God, one Creator, one Father; therefore, we consider ourselves, all the gifts we have received, all our capacities and material gifts as granted in view of God's entire family. We then believe that we can rejoice in our unique name, our capacities and all that we have only to the extent that we commit ourselves to our neighbor and to the community. We believe in one Lord Jesus Christ who came not to please himself but to be a servant for all men. Therefore, we believe that there is no salvation for us in Christ unless we too commit ourselves with him for the whole world and for a saving community. We can be rescued from the dark powers of evil, i.e., from the pernicious solidarity of egotists, only if we too, like Christ, make ourselves servants

of salvation in brotherly solidarity. He is born of the
Virgin Mary, the humble maiden who pleases God by her
humility, her willingness to serve and her constant Magnificat that his Church may follow her example. We believe that Christ has borne the burden of all, has taken
upon himself the heavy load of the past in order to transform it and to give it new meaning. So we too believe
that even the evil in our world can be transformed by us
into a saving power if we bear the burdens of one another
in the same spirit as Jesus Christ.

We believe that Christ gave his body to be the bread
for the life of the world. Beholding his sacrifice, the
Father revealed him as the Lord; the Father gave witness
to him by raising him from the dead. We believe, therefore, that we will find our true selves and attain fulfillment by giving ourselves to neighbor and to community
for the life of the world. We believe in the one Holy
Spirit, the Giver of all good gifts; therefore, all our hope
reposes in solidarity if, in redeemed love, we deploy all
our gifts and God-given charisms for the building up of
the one body in Christ. We believe in one holy Catholic
Church; therefore, in receiving the body of Christ, we
recommit ourselves again and again to a constant conversion so as to become more fully the body of Christ and
to strive untiringly toward Christian unity so that the
Church may become more visibly a sacrament of unity
for the whole of mankind. We believe in the one baptism
which Christ endured for all; therefore we are baptized
into solidarity and we know it will be a saving event for
us if we live accordingly. Therefore, in the one hope
that is held out for us, we look forward to the resurrection
from the dead in the communion of the saints, to the
concelebration of God's triune love.

The Creed implies both grateful acceptance of the
joyous News and response on our part; it thus calls for a

commitment to salvific truth in love and trust. It infers solidarity of the community of believers in hope and a hope in solidarity based on the salvific truth in Christ who is Truth and Solidarity incarnate and thus our hope and the hope of the whole world. Faith is an existential event through which man receives liberation, that is, freedom in truth with a commitment to work for the true liberation of all. Through salvific faith, man emerges from the prison of his lonely selfishness and collective prejudice. Faith entails a commitment to solidarity in Christ; it also serves to liberate effectively from original sin and from solidarity in selfishness.

We can now see that faith in Christ is totally different from any kind of "religion" that indulges in speculation about the number of angelic choirs, about the principle of individuation with respect to angels, or whether the *hymen virginale* of Mary was preserved in its physical integrity when she gave birth to Jesus and so on. Faith is not the alienation of an other-worldly hope conceived as some romantic I-Thou oasis where we can be alone with "sweet Jesus" and no longer disturbed by the noise and clamor of our brothers and sisters. Christian faith and hope looking forward to life after death and the world to come are the strongest possible motives for a common recommitment to God's world, for furthering the solidarity of mankind here and now. A faithful response to salvation truth fully utilizes all present opportunities for the honor of the One Creator and Redeemer and for the good of all his children.

Faith inevitably leads to a deeper understanding of the yearning of the created universe for freedom. Since salvation is all-embracing, the believer knows that he cannot escape the dark powers of original sin, that is, selfishness, collective injustice and prejudices, power structures and violence, unless he entrenches himself in the one hope that comes from Christ. For Christ's sake, he feels compelled to unite himself with all men of good will for the building up of a better world. This commitment to God's world in faith and hope must distinguish the witness of the Church as the community of faith and love. For only then can the Church effectively become a visible sign of hope, a sacrament of unity for the whole of mankind, as Vatican II's *Lumen gentium* proposes in its very first article. It is through this solidarity, this saving event, this commitment and this response to the rallying call that we escape from solidarity in evil and become the great sign of hope for all humanity.

The pilgrim Church, faithful to the Bible and to her tradition, links together everything that God has done with new events. In her faith, she sees tradition as a current of life calling for growth, constant searching and meditation. God is still working, as Christ pointedly told the priests and Pharisees, the rear-guard of the Church of Israel: "My Father has never yet ceased to work, and I am working too" (Jn. 5:17). Truly God is reposing, is enjoying his sabbath. He is always the same, but this does not preclude his constantly revealing himself throughout history in new manifestations, particularly through those who put into practice his words.

The hope basis of faith serves to orient the Church's moral teaching toward a more dynamic understanding of the Sermon on the Mount, more specifically toward the sevenfold "But I tell you . . ."; all injunctions point to the goal commandment: "be all goodness just as your heavenly Father is all goodness," "love your enemies as God the Father who sends his rain and sunshine for the just and the unjust." Love expressed in great gratitude, generosity, creativity and openness is also related to the directive: "God's own will be done on earth as it is in heaven."

The law of faith represents a call to growth. Vigilance

and hope help man see the next step whereas faith urges him constantly to set out, never resting content with himself, but to seek the path of salvation according to the gift bestowed upon him by Christ (Eph. 4:7), according to present opportunities. God's design is clearly one of love for the transformation of the whole world throughout history according to the pattern of love he manifested in Christ. He sends the Holy Spirit so that his salvation plan will be carried out till all things are fulfilled.

7
THE SACRAMENTALITY OF HOPE

Since God's original design for man becomes visible in Christ and all things are made through him and for him, they are visible and effective signs of hope for the believer. We can and should therefore speak of an all-embracing sacramental character of hope, but sacramentality understood in a broad sense. The well-known Orthodox professor of theology A. Schmemann of St. Vladimir's Seminary has written a book about the sacramentality of creation[1]; the work is biblical and in our best tradition. The whole of creation is, according to him, a sacrament, a perceptible sign of God's presence and fidelity because it is turned toward Christ who is the fully visible sign of God's presence.

Throughout the billions of years of evolution since the creation of the universe, God's constant attention directs everything toward hominization and finally toward the point Omega, Christ Jesus, the great sign of his love. The whole evolutionary process evinces God's gracious presence steering everything toward the fullness of time, the

[1] A. Schmemann, *Sacraments and Orthodoxy* (New York: Herder and Herder, 1965).

complete divulgence of his salvific plan. By creating man
and woman in his likeness, he fashions them in view of
the full image of himself which he will manifest in Christ.

We must evidently move away from a mere churchly
view of sacraments for this would conceal God's word
and work. God also communicates hope in the secular
world, indeed, in the whole of creation. Since he is present
everywhere, he expresses his design in all his works in
view of the final revelation of his Word who is to become
flesh. When Christ comes, he speaks him out, he who is
the great Sacrament; and through him, God expresses
himself in many sacraments, i.e., in all events, in all his
words and deeds which make manifest the hope that the
Father gives us in him. By healing the sick, by feeding
the hungry, by receiving the outcast, by giving sight to
the blind, by siding with the victims of discrimination, he
gives us sacraments, visible signs for the greater message
of eternal life. What Christ does and says is a full "word,"
a sign of hope for the whole person and not just for the
soul. It becomes a salvific sign to have hope for a healthier, more humane and just world within the context of
greater hope for eternal life.

Throughout his earthly life, Christ gave many signs of
hope and some of them were shocking. Hope of this kind
was unknown to the priestly class. When Christ entered
into humble dialogue with the woman from Samaria asking for water to drink and promised her even better water, "an inner spring always welling up for eternal life"
(Jn. 4:14), he makes use of common everyday things:
water, the well of Jacob and objects related to the
quenching of thirst. Thus they become signs of that better
water for which man thirsts, namely, everlasting life. He
touches her own misery: the man with whom she is living
is not her husband; she has had five and yet for this
woman there is hope: "I can see you are a prophet"

(Jn. 4:19). She can say publicly and without bitterness: "Come see the man who has told me everything I ever did. Could this be the Messiah?" (Jn. 4:29). In this unusual encounter, we find no frustration; Christ grants forgiveness and inspires hope.

A woman known as a sinner in the city, probably Mary Magdalen, likewise becomes one of the great signs of hope through Jesus Christ. The Pharisees despised her: "If this fellow were a real prophet he would know who this woman is that touches him and what sort of woman she is, a sinner" (Lk. 7:39). Yet the Lord gives her great encouragement by assuring her that she will love with that pure and grateful love which corresponds to the fullness of the mercy she receives. Not only is she a sign of hope but also the great apostle of hope on Easter morning. She who had been known as a public sinner has the privilege of bringing the message of the resurrection even to Peter and John.

Again, Christ is the great sign of hope for the woman caught in adultery. According to the Code of Hammurabi written about 1900 B.C., only the woman caught in adultery was to be stoned; the man went free. In the Code of Moses, both adulterous parties had to be punished but this arrogant Pharisee group brought only the woman to punishment. For her, there was no mercy; she had to be stoned. In a salvific gesture, Christ writes in the sand the sins of those righteous men and invites them: "The one among you who is without sin shall throw the first stone at her" (Jn. 8:7). His mercy is saving judgment, an invitation to mercy and to conversion: "No one has condemned you?"—"No one, sir" she said. Jesus replied: "No more do I. Go in peace, but do not sin again" (Jn. 8: 10–11).

All of Christ's encounters were pledges of hope. Christ, our hope, is the great and unique sacrament of hope. All the other sacraments, all other events and signs, receive their meaning in him, in view of him, the One who was, is and will come. He is the One who is constantly coming, for he is with his pilgrim Church and through her he turns our hope to his final coming and to the here-and-now. He is coming for the world in evolution, a world in the grip of tension, a world called to judgment but finally to hope. When Christ does return, when he will hand everything and himself over to the Father, he will no longer be a sacrament of hope. He will then be the fulfillment for all who have put their hope in him. Meanwhile, he is the One who has come, who is coming and who will come; he is a sacrament of hope for those who are looking for his coming.

Through Christ, the pilgrim Church is a sacrament of hope and a great sacrament, but she is not automatically so in all her parts and members. She is a sacrament of hope to the extent that she accepts her role as a Church on the march, that she is ready to change and ready for that salvific discontinuity that restores her credibility as a sign of hope. She is a sign of hope if she confesses her sins and does so all over the world: "Forgive us our trespasses as we forgive those who have trespassed against us."

The Church is a sacrament of hope insofar as she is the mother of mercy. Where the Church in her teachings, in the utterances of her theologians and bishops, assumes a rigoristic stance, she is no longer a sacrament of hope but becomes a sacrament of pessimism and despair. Jansenism did not proclaim hope; it radiated the frustration of a rigoristic, merciless Church, a Church for the so-called "holy ones" who were self-righteous but not saintly. God, the Holy One, is merciful. The Church is a great sign of mercy in the sacramental sense of Mary who stands under the cross. She is a sacrament of hope to the extent that she is understanding and realizes that even for herself, hope is an undeserved gift. She cannot proclaim her own triumphs; she proclaims the mercy of God when she models herself on the image, the prototype, the handmaid Mary, following Christ, the merciful and humble servant Messiah. Then only can she be an effective and credible sign of hope.

So the Church is one of sinners and for sinners who are striving toward holiness in mercy and in gratitude. It is only through her faith in God's gracious mercy for all men that she can have hope. How could she possibly hope in God, trust in God if she is merciless toward certain categories of men? Those who have been graced with five talents, who have a deep knowledge of God and his mercy, should they be hard and merciless for others who have barely received one talent? How can they truly trust in God? How can they be a sign of hope?

The Church is a sacrament, a visible and credible sign of hope when, like Abraham leaving behind his homeland and his family, she looks forward trustfully, or when, like Moses and his people who left behind the security and slavery of Egypt, she sets out into an uncertain future. Similarly, Lot left behind him the city to be destroyed and set out for the unknown. In some of her members, however, the Church calls down upon herself the Lord's warning: "Remember the wife of Lot" (Lk. 17:32). Those who are constantly weeping and looking back to the "good old days" are likely to become petrified monuments of pessimism. They cling to traditions which no longer express the presence of a living God and his concern for today's people; their traditions become museum pieces and a graveyard without hope. Hope cannot be displayed in museums, for hope is life.

The Church is a sacrament of hope as a pilgrim Church setting out into the future, leaving behind all false and all too human securities, to entrust herself fully to God, the Lord and Redeemer of history. The Church is a sacrament of hope if she courageously undertakes a thorough and painstaking soul searching to eliminate whatever is an encumbrance on her pilgrim journey. In the Constantinian era, some of the Church's institutions were not only understandable but also useful; however, were she to cling to these outdated structures today, the Church would only be a sign of frustration and despair. What is still useful, what is still serviceable from tradition, should be preserved. God's own word is always life and spirit, but it has to be translated into a new context.

Where Church structures cause only frustration because of an institutionalized suspicion revealing itself in too many controls, there is an apparent lack of trust in God. On the other hand, when people refuse every kind of human authority or guidelines, they are more confident in themselves than trusting in God. We need a healthy distrust with regard to our own weaknesses; it is a part of our trust in God, but the latter must always be greater than our distrust of human weakness. Whenever the order is reversed, we have demonology. It is a question of proportion; God is infinitely greater than all weaknesses and all the powers of darkness.

A Church in the process of reform, which is becoming more aware of her imperfections and yearns for a more thoroughgoing renewal, is one that inspires hope in spite of the fact that she may yet be wanting in many respects. This is the situation in the Church today; she has a greater awareness of her own shortcomings and of her need for reform. She is gaining a keener and more penetrating vision of God's grace, and this is a sign of hope.

When the Church is in need of reform but becomes complacent, apologetic or defensive, she then becomes a countersacrament; take for example, the senseless and useless series of titles or the long ceremonial trains of the cardinals, which are now much shorter but still outrageously expensive. Last year when I was in Sicily attending the Congress of Marriage Counselors, there happened to be an exhibit of rare animals just outside our meeting hall. I was intrigued by a strange-looking animal whose tail was much longer than the body and I asked one of the priests: "What's the name of that animal?" Surprised, he asked in turn: "Don't you know? That's a cardinal!" We must cultivate a sense of humor as regards our weaknesses; it is a sign that we still have hope. We should gratefully acknowledge to God that many cardinals and bishops now live in a style of apostolic simplicity. They stand poles apart from the Renaissance cardinals. Many are working for even more radical reforms.

An outdated canon law is not a sign of hope. However, in spite of its obsoleteness, we have here a sign of hope if people in the Church strive to serve the Lord and do not allow themselves to transgress God's all-important law of love in favor of outmoded canons. If a serious effort is made to revise and adjust it to the needs of modern man and in the light of present opportunities, there is a basis for hope.

There are still many power blocs and critic clubs, people who encourage bitterness and who radiate so much frustration that they are strengthened in it; they personify pessimism. They do not constitute the whole Church; however, it is possible to be blinded by an army of pessimists. We honor God when we give the greater attention to joyous celebrations and to the courageous initiatives of those who spread joy and peace with their good sense of humor.

There is a Church of saints, of the humble, of the open-minded, of learners, of those who do penance, of those who forgive as God has forgiven them—and they are really the Church as a visible sign of God's mercy. Before becoming alarmed and angered by the unpleasant stream of pessimists, we must search for and find God's presence; he never leaves man without hope. A Church in need of reform is a stumbling block if she is not ready to change, but a Church that finds itself in such a tremendous process of reform and renewal as ours is in a normal pilgrim situation. Because of this effort, because of this humble avowal of her need for change, she is a sacrament of hope. All those who want to anticipate the heavenly Jerusalem, who do not want to be a part of the pilgrim Church confessing: "Forgive us our trespasses"— they are bound to be scandalized by the present status of the Church.

The believer should always be both happy and unhappy about his Church, but happiness should predominate. He praises God for keeping alive and bringing new life to his Church. She is hopefully on the way toward reform; for this we must be grateful while remaining fully aware of our own need for redemption and renewal, and of the need of the whole Church to become more consciously a pilgrim Church, one which is imperfect yet accepts the call to holiness with increasing vigilance for the present opportunities. The Church, in her very imperfections and limitations which will always be a part of her life in time, is a prognostic sign, as the Church Fathers used to say, a sign directing our hopes toward the life beyond present history while strengthening our energies as we move toward the fullness of life.

History offers hope in the saints, the converts, the humble people, those who remain alert in a life of prayer and service to the poor; yet, these numbers do not allow us to confuse the earthly with the heavenly Jerusalem. We are longing and yearning for the heavenly Jerusalem. We must therefore learn humility and understand Christian life as constant conversion and renewal.

In Christian hope, there is always a prophetic element, a protest against what falls short of God's graciousness, what does not respond to the call for a more painstaking examination of conscience or greater readiness for conversion. There is a sign of hope in the prophetic dissent, in the live protest of those who are in full solidarity with the Church. In non-violent, prophetic protest there is no passive resignation. Those who carry on this kind of protest will never be heard referring to hopeless people or hopeless situations because they always stand ready to contribute a worthy effort.

Whereas criticism without hope or initiatives for change can spell frustration and bitterness, there is such a thing as criticism inspired by love and accompanied by deeds looking toward new horizons; this is a sign of hope and it deserves credit. A futile criticism wastes time lamenting bad structures, outdated laws and backlashes; such critics remain unconcerned about their own conversion and the possibility of their contributing to a better climate in the Church. Only those parts of the Church equally concerned with the reform of structures and their personal conversion honor God and inspire hope in others. They are genuinely mindful of the need for a better world and for more holy people; in the fullest sense, therefore, they constitute a veritable sign or sacrament of hope.

If the Church wants to be continually and ever more fully a sacrament of hope, she has to overcome all security complexes. Realism must enter the picture; for example, since we have to deal with different kinds of people, there is need for different types of religious congregations; we need conservative groups that can provide a home for people in great need of security. However, the whole Church should not be turned into a home for insecure people. If we need mental asylums for sick people, we cannot expect the whole Church to become such an institution. There must be room for different characters and many temperaments, but the Church must not be crippled by the insecurity that seeks to guarantee unity through a uniform canon law or an inflexible liturgy that would not allow for spontaneity. In spite of the fact that Latin has gone out as the uniform language in liturgy, we have not yet rooted out the mentality that seeks unity through the imposition of one language and mode of thinking on Christians of all cultures.

Newsmen have approached me recently inquiring about what kind of changes I would make in Church structures if I had my way; they questioned pointedly: Would you do away with monsignori and cardinals? I replied firmly in the negative at which they seem startled; however, I qualified my answer by saying that I would see to it that people interested in these titles knew exactly what they meant. I would suggest one canon reading: "Any priest who indulges in vanity has a right to be named monsignor and to call himself 'the very right and reverend monsignor.' If he can prove his ineptitude for anything else, he is entitled to become a super-monsignor; however, he would have to pay half of his salary to the missions for such a privilege. He would be allowed to wear any color of vestments but never in holy places; he would have to promise not to get angry at people who are amused by his vanity." As for the cardinals, I would do something similar. The conditions would be that he must be at least eighty years of age to be nominated; it would have to be proved that he is incapable of new initiatives, etc. The conditions could be stated in such a way that no great churchman would honestly ever aspire to such positions and titles. It follows that the election of the successor of St. Peter would no longer be in the hands of men over eighty. In my opinion, the various grades of monsignori and the institution of the cardinalate are signs of an outdated era. However, new things are emerging; we can afford to smile at certain remnants of the Church's triumphalistic age.

There is a problem in the Church today and we must confront it realistically; we need room for old people; there must be some place of honor where they can retire. For example, in Rome we have the chapters of the Canons of St. Mary Major and of St. John Lateran; these institutions are good in the sense that some recognition is given to people who would no longer be capable of occupying an active post. Here they can be promoted and will no longer interfere with progress. This represents a concession to human weakness; everyone knows that many of these canons cannot function adequately in responsible positions but they would not be happy without honors, titles and ostentatious vestments. Again, a sense of humor helps us cope with human frailty.

However, when such structures are intimated as being the very core of the Church, when they receive serious attention and wide publicity, they then become a source of frustration. Knowing that we are in a period of transition can help us focus on the positive signs with a strong sense of trust in God and that sense of humor that allows us to detect all of today's new signs of hope. We are then in a position to deal more realistically with problems because of the promising signs of hope; God's presence in his Church and his promise never to let it down sustain our hope.

The Church is a sacrament of hope, but we must never forget that Christ alone is the basis of our hope, the true sacrament of hope. All the other realities are visible and effective signs only to the extent that they direct our attention and trust completely to Christ.

A great deal of frustration is bound to arise when one's trust rests solely in the institutional aspect of the Church. The prophetic element is then obscured giving rise to disillusionment and disappointment. A right understanding of the Church should include the following points: (1) it should turn all our hope toward God in Christ Jesus; (2) it should not underestimate the prophetic-charismatic element in the Church and (3) it should pay attention to God's ongoing action in the world. If so often we are deeply disappointed in our churchmen or in the Church itself, it is because we have placed all our hope in them or are victims of shortsightedness. The sacramentality of the Church and of all created things can only have meaning if it leads to greater trust in God, and in God alone. The officeholder in the Church is certainly entitled to trust and confidence but he is bound by the human predicament; absolute trust can be lodged in God alone.

Feelings of despair and bitterness stemming from institutional weaknesses and the faults of men belonging to the "system" are often due to a narrow concept of the Church. In the Church there are many ministries and charisms. Officeholders may occasionally give a wrong impression by seeming to be identified with the Church as an institution or with authority. If the Church of the Old and of the New Testament is to become a sign of hope, it will be particularly through the prophetic men and women whom God sends us in his mercy. When we try to envision the unity of all the various ministries, we realize that healthy conflicts arising temporarily are necessary growing pains much like the pangs of childbirth.

Just as officeholders in the Church must not think of themselves as "the Church," similarly the Church as a whole must never give the impression that she monopolizes the actions of God in the world. She is more genuinely a sign of hope if she opens her eyes to all the good God performs through various men the world over throughout history.

The Synod of Bishops meeting every other year in Rome is a tremendous sign of hope. The fact that Pope Paul, after serious discussion and considerable opposition, agreed to have the world episcopate select permanent advisers for the secretariat of the Synod, and that the bishops will have an active voice with regard to the agenda of the meetings, are both great signs of hope, signs that new structures are replacing the old ones.

8

THE SACRAMENTS OF CHRISTIAN HOPE

The broader concept of sacramentality in the Church and the world inevitably leads us to the seven sacraments of the Church which are often referred to as "sacraments of faith" or "sacraments of hope." A vision of sacramentality which extends to all the signs of God's presence helps us to a better appreciation of the seven sacraments because it awakens trust in him, invites us to feel grateful for his gifts and makes men instruments of peace and hope. This is the perspective in which these privileged signs of hope ought to be presented in an enlightened cate-chesis.

The idea has been classically expressed by St. Augus-tine in his response to the question: How can the sacra-ments be signs of salvation when we keep them from the heathen? He replied by pointing to the cross of the Re-deemer where we find the mystery of the hidden God effectively revealing his infinite love. "With deep roots and on firm foundation, may you be strong to grasp, with all God's people, what is the breadth, length, height and depth of the love of Christ. Perhaps this is the cross of our Lord. There is the breadth of the arms stretched out to all; there is the depth which gives firmness to the whole cross where all the hope of our life stands firmly rooted. Then the breadth will not be lacking in our good deeds where there is the length of perseverance unto the end. The good deeds have their height when the heart dwells above with Christ, so that in their full length and breadth of goodness all the good deeds arise from the hope of the heavenly reward. The height means that we do not look for an earthly remuneration so that it will not be said of us 'they already have their reward' (Mt. 6:2). The depth, as already stated, is that hidden part of the cross rooted in the earth which gives it support and firmness so that all can see it. But what is that hidden part, I mean, what is hidden in the Church? I reply: the sacrament of baptism and the sacrament of the eucharist. But while the sacraments remain hidden to the heathen, they can see your good deeds. What is visible arises from that depth which they cannot perceive much like the hidden part of the cross that rises and is visible."[1]

St. Augustine thus envisions the celebration and reception of the sacraments in their essential dynamism toward life. The faithful who live according to the gift and mission imparted to them through the sacraments become visible signs of hope and salvation for those who do not know the sacraments. The sacraments prove to be signs of hope for us if, through them, we come to know Christ better and reveal him by our witness. In other words, we truly accept the grace and mission of the sacraments if, in turn, we become "sacraments," visible and efficacious signs of hope for the world around us.

In order to enter more fully into the biblical perspective and the great vision of the earlier centuries, we must strive to free ourselves from an all too technical concept

[1] Augustine, *En. in Psalmum CIII*, PL 37, 348.

of the sacraments; they must not be looked upon as a "sacramental system" with inflexible rules. It is helpful to recall that the Church herself could be a sacrament and celebrate the sacraments for eleven centuries without ever attempting to count their number. It was Peter Lombard in the twelfth century who first stated that the Church had seven and only seven sacraments. This theologian remained, for centuries, very influential even beyond his merits due to the fact that the works of Thomas Aquinas had been placed on the Index of Forbidden Books by the archbishop of Paris and remained practically unavailable until the sixteenth century.

It must be acknowledged that Peter Lombard used good criteria in determining the number seven: a sacrament had to be a salvific sign instituted by Christ for all time and for all his disciples for the good of the whole Church. Before his day, however, almost all treatises on the sacraments included the washing of feet because Christ had washed the feet of his apostles; it was also a common practice for many centuries. As a liturgical rite, however, the custom was considered a sacrament only when the participants thereby committed themselves to Christ, the Servant. The actual rite was regarded as fruitful sacrament only if the person subsequently rendered humble service to whoever needed it. Whenever, through God's gracious presence, his kindness and mercy appeal to man's heart, we have a sacrament in the broader sense of the term.

From its earliest days the Church celebrated the sacraments as living signs of faith, gratitude and hope. Validity had not yet become a technical problematic, but no sacrament would have made sense to Christians if it had not been a sign of hope inspiring them to even greater hope and trust. One of the reasons for this hope lay in the very fact that the sacraments as instituted by Christ had

definite promises associated with them. Whenever we
celebrate them in accord with the intent of Christ, we receive another new assurance of his goodness, mercy and
fidelity; we become transformed into ever more visible
signs of hope for the world around us. The celebration
and reception of the sacraments in the community of
hope transfigures the participants into signs of solidarity
in hope and hope in salvific solidarity. That is why the
sacraments can be called a privileged school of hope.

The sacraments are manifestations of God's graciousness, of his attractive countenance turning to man. Each
sacrament then becomes an interpersonal encounter of
man with God. The relationship is established through
God's initiative, his undeserved goodness, kindness and
mercy. Insofar as Christians accept the sacraments as
God's benevolent initiative and appreciate them as God's
gifts, to that extent they are on the way to becoming outstanding signs of hope. As sanctifying events, they constitute a new perspective for and add new dimensions to
the most basic human experiences. When presenting the
sacraments and explaining their celebration as a great
sign of hope, it is most important that the liturgical ceremony clearly indicate their dynamism with respect to
personal and communal life.

With this frame of reference, we can now proceed to
consider the seven sacraments in turn. We are to look
upon them as privileged signs of hope, a privileged school
of hope and of all the other eschatological virtues which
will be treated later.

As an efficacious sign of hope in solidarity, *baptism*
derives its proper dimension from Christ's own baptism.
In the Gospel of St. Luke, we read that Christ was baptized by St. John the Baptist during a general baptism. At
that moment, the heavens opened, the Spirit came visibly
upon him and the voice of the Father was heard saying:

"Thou art my Son, my Beloved; on thee my favor rests" (Lk. 3:22). Christ presented himself in a crowd of tax-gatherers ready to make restitution, among soldiers who had been blackmailing others, among prostitutes and similar unclean people who knew they were poor but who hoped for redemption. The Pharisees were not present. During the general baptism of people very much aware of their need for forgiveness, Christ presented himself to make known that he was bearing their burdens, thus revealing the meaning of his cross as the great baptism. In the same Gospel, Christ refers to his death on the cross: "I have a baptism to undergo, and how hampered I am until the ordeal is over" (Lk. 12:50). We can say that Christ was baptized in his own blood for all men, "to set fire to the earth" (Lk. 12:49), preparing the new earth and the new heaven where love and unity will reign.

Baptism introduces us to the hope-inspiring reality that Christ really bears our burden, that by his life blood he calls us to become his brothers and sisters. He invites and receives us in the saving solidarity manifested in the ritual baptism in the Jordan and in the life-blood baptism, i.e., in the liturgy and in life and death. So it means insertion into the community of salvation with Christ who has freed us from deleterious solidarity in sinfulness. As members of the community of faith, we are now sharers in the gladdening News. As members of the community of hope, we are committed to the building up of a better milieu, one promoting a more humane and faithful life. We are effectively inserted into the community of hope when we in turn become initiators of hope, having first received the undeserved sign of hope. We are destined to become ever greater signs of hope throughout the course of our lives. That baptism is a sign of hope should be made specially visible in its mode of celebration; all per-

sons in attendance should be made to realize that by
being baptized into saving solidarity with Christ, into the
body of Christ, we are directing ourselves toward the
eucharist, the great sign of unity and preparing for a life
in accord with these two great signs of hope.

The *eucharist,* the central experience of faith, expresses
the waiting in joyful expectation for the coming of our
Savior Jesus Christ. Since it is a "sacrament," it should become visible in the way in which it is celebrated, moving
both heart and mind of the concelebrants. We may therefore ask: What kind of sacrament would a eucharistic
celebration be where no joy and hope come through,
where no encouragement is received? The eucharist is the
great sign of the baptism of Christ who opens his arms to
all, giving hope to all; it is awaiting his blessed coming in
the community of the hopeful, the joyful expectancy of
the pilgrim Church.

It follows that a priest capable of concelebrating mass
with his confrères but who insists on celebrating "the visible sign of unity" in splendid isolation becomes a counter-
sign. I am not referring to priests who are incarcerated
and cannot concelebrate or others who are psychologically incapacitated. The offender is he who does not like
the community of others and who, therefore, in his self-
imposed isolation, celebrates original sin. He does not
meet Christ as a sign of hope and solidarity for the community and in the community. His celebration is not the
sacrament that manifests to others or brings to his personal life any promise of hope. Concelebration, however,
only makes sense if the gracious command of brotherhood and solidarity is overtly acknowledged and recon-
firmed. We are called to concelebrate God's love with all
God's people and to yearn for the oneness of the priestly
people of God and the ministerial priesthood.

A loveless celebration fails to be a sacrament truly

and fully, that is, a visible sign of hope. It would be helpful if occasionally we were to ask ourselves: What does
Christ want me to do as a pilgrim coming to him? The
eucharist can alert us to his coming in daily events while
we await his final coming.

The eucharist underscores all the dimensions of our
faith by bringing to the fore our gratitude for all the
great signs of hope given in the past: the creation, the
incarnation, Christ's death and ascension and the mission
of the Holy Spirit. Our personal experiences are also to be
brought to the eucharist so that all together, with everything that we share, we can look forward in a community
of faith and hope to the final coming of the Lord.

Confirmation is the sacrament of growth toward maturity in docility to the Spirit. It is a sign of hope through
which Christ calls us insistently to the blessed freedom of
the sons and daughters of God. It signifies the fullness of
time when we allow ourselves to be led by the Spirit, the
giver of all good gifts. Thus we regain a mature perspective on Christian life and open ourselves to the needs
of others, being vigilant always for the present opportunities. The Spirit frees us from selfish concern and makes
us instruments of peace and justice, signs of hope for
many. It assimilates us to Christ "who did not consider
himself." Consecrated by his Spirit, "each of us must consider his neighbor and think what is for his good and will
build up the common life" (Rom. 15:2).

For adults coming to faith, the sacrament of confirmation constitutes a part of the total celebration of initiation
into the community of faith and hope. It is a commitment
to solidarity through the consecration by the Spirit in
whom Christ dedicated himself for his brethren. In the
case of infant baptism, it seems advisable to postpone
reception of confirmation until the age of initiation into
the adult world and public life. The choice of one's own

state of life and profession should be cast in the light of this sacrament of hope in mature solidarity.

Most ancient cultures had a formal initiation ceremony for young people. It was most appropriate that the sacrament of confirmation be related to this decisive social and personal event. Particularly in Africa, initiation rites had and to some extent still have an extraordinary relevance in terms of the assumption of social responsibilities. In many tribes, initiation provided a very strong psychological and religious motivation for premarital chastity and other important social virtues. Unfortunately, in many parts of Africa, the missionaries displayed hostility toward the whole idea of initiation and by doing away with it, deprived the African people of a precious inherited and much needed psychological and social support. Instead, they should have followed the example of the early Church and looked at the traditional initiation rite in the full light of confirmation.

Confirmation fulfills the hopes and promises expressed by the traditional initiation ceremonies and it should be made a sign of genuine continuity. Since initiation is an important feature of tribal and family life, preparation for confirmation and its celebration should strive to integrate all the good from the past and thus pave the way for the future. Where Christian faith has taken deeper roots it would not be too difficult to restore and revitalize the initiation rites with a view to promoting the growth not only of the individual but also of the community and culture.

The sacrament of *reconciliation* makes clear to man that he is the beneficiary of God's undeserved shalom. God's peace comes to him but he receives it only if he accepts the call to be transformed into a messenger of peace and if he is shaped by God's own forgiveness and can forgive others. The Christian receives it best and is

aware of having received it when he becomes a visible
and effective sign of peace and reconciliation for others on
all levels.

The sacrament of reconciliation, or shalom, should be
the outstanding personal experience of God's mercy in
the Church and through the Church also intended to be
a real experience of compassion and mercy. But when a
person enters a dark box and is separated by a partition
behind which a tiger is growling, how can the sacrament
of peace be visible? A sacramental celebration involving
a depersonalized being who relies heavily on casuistic
solutions which he applies mechanically to an unknown
and unseen person cannot possibly be in harmony with
Christ's intent. The very meaning of "visible sign" com-
pels the Church to reform its practices and to renew the
mode of celebrating the sacrament in a way that will
speak to the man of today.

Marriage is a sacrament, a visible sign of an experience
of hope to the extent that the spouses trust each other,
faithfully keep their promises and forgive one another.
The juridical marriage contract by itself, if it is not followed by a covenant of love, can become more of a cause
of despair than a sign of hope. But marriage vows expressed after serious preparation and in all sincerity can
be pledges inspiring a deeper understanding of God's
promise in the new and everlasting covenant. We must
not minimize the fact that an effective sacramentality of
marriage depends on the degree to which hope and trust,
kindness and mutual understanding become visible.

A few years ago, I was speaking about marriage validity and asked those present which of two cases they
would consider to be more of a sacrament. The responses
varied and some were quite contradictory. The first case
involved a mixed marriage declared invalid because the
pastor, refusing to grant the dispensation, obliged the

couple to have the marriage celebrated in the Lutheran Church. Canonically, the marriage was invalid; however, these two persons loved each other dearly, prayed together, helped one another draw closer to God and were the first messengers of the Gospel to their children. After fifty years when the marriage was being canonically validated, the priest asked: "Mr. Miller, do you accept Miss Schneider as your valid spouse?"

The second case involved a marriage which met all the canonical regulations; the priest spent two hours looking for impediments and found none. The marriage was then celebrated according to the proper rules. However, these two people never cared for each other, never prayed together, never shared a word about God. On the contrary, they consistently frustrated one another. Where is the sacrament?

Of course, there is something lacking in the first case but lacking chiefly on the part of that canonist or priest who locked the institutional door. But the Holy Spirit is not hampered by human mishandling. It is through God's gift and man's generous response that a marriage does become a sacrament.

The way the Church today draws the line between valid and invalid marriages creates a distressing problem in many parts of the world but particularly in Africa where the cultures cannot understand the Mediterranean formulation of canon law. In numerous tribes, if the marriage is not blessed with children after two or three years, it is torn asunder by the clan, whether the spouses like it or not. Both families are eager to disprove that sterility is on their side. Frequently both partners in second marriages can boast of having as many as ten or twelve children and live happily together. If the first marriage was blessed in the Church, most of the diocesan officials consider it indissoluble in spite of the fact that the condition "if it becomes fertile" is deeply written in the whole culture and in the heart and mind of the contracting parties. Some priests tend to encourage a canonical celebration of the marriage only after children are born; meanwhile, they exclude these spouses from the sacraments because in their eyes these people are living in plain fornication. Others bless the first marriage but give no hope to those who, after their marriage is dissolved, live in a second stable marriage. But is not their new family life with all the love, fidelity, forbearance, good education of the children, a sign of hope in the perspective of salvation?

A priest in Africa told me a few years ago: "I have 23,000 Catholics and they are all religious people. If I were to observe all the rules of canon law, I would have to excommunicate 80 per cent of them. However, I refuse to do so; I look to their good will. I cannot possibly go through all the details of canonical legislation; I have 2000 catechumens and only one assistant. Were I to heed all canonical processes for marriage, I would be a frustrated administrator with no time to preach the Gospel."

I do not deny the right of the Church to lay down certain rules for determining the validity of marriages. However, the emphasis must not be one-sidedly on canonical validity; greater attention should be given to whether each marriage becomes truly, in daily life, an effective sign of hope. This requires a more careful preparation for marriage and a constant concern for the spouses' growth in marital love. During the celebration of the sacrament and throughout their married lives, the spouses should learn to link their hope for everlasting life with their marriage covenant. It is God who entrusts them to each other and remains with them so that they can love each other with a redeemed and redeeming love. They cannot expect absolute and final beatitude in their marriage; therefore,

they will not be so frustrated when their illusions collapse
and they have to bear with their mutual weaknesses.
Hope in God's forbearance will inspire a generous readiness to forgive. Marriage is a school of hope if the spouses
learn together to put all their hope in God and to view
their mutual trust only as a puzzling mirror-image of
their confidence in him. If they love each other in spite of
all their weaknesses and failures, they will grow in understanding of God's undeserved and tender love.

The irrevocable commitment sanctioned by the Church
and celebrated before the Church is a beginning, a sign
of hope that God will fulfill what he has begun if they
pray and co-operate with his grace. It is not primarily
the canonical sanctions but rather the inner power of
God's grace, coupled with their mutual love graced by
trust in God, that guarantees effectively the indissolu-
bility of their covenant.

The Church's canonical regulations on marriage and
her pastoral solicitude are a sign of hope if she blends
the call to fidelity with demonstrable understanding, compassion and mercy. The Church cannot proclaim reconciliation to that person who has deserted his spouse leaving him/her waiting for the return unless the culprit does
his best to seek reconciliation. However, in cases where
the first marriage can in no way be restored, if we find
absolute good will in people living in a canonically invalid marriage which, notwithstanding, bears the marks
of love, commitment and dedication, there must be a
serious effort on the part of the Church to manifest herself and her sacraments as signs of hope.

In a number of cases there is ample evidence that the
first marriage never truly deserved the name of "sacrament" and even canonically it was not valid. I cannot see
why, in such cases, pastors and confessors should co-
operate so fully with those canonists who demand 101

per cent proof for the invalidity of the first marriage
while, with less than 1 per cent proof, they turn these
people away from the sacraments of the Church. We
will return later to this burning question that has so much
to do with the right understanding of the Church and her
sacraments as signs of hope for all men of good will.

Here I wish to offer only one suggestion with regard
to so-called "insoluble marriage cases." I often counsel
such couples as follows: "Although I cannot do anything
to get your marriage into the parish registers, I advise
you to pray together and do your best to make your
present marriage a true sign of love and of hope, a community of faith. Be signs of hope and of God's own love
for your children. Be faithful to one another. If your love
becomes more and more redeemed and profound, you
may consider this a sign that God is graciously present
to you and is giving you hope." My position may seem
strange to some, but I believe that through God's grace,
a marriage can become very much an effective sign of
grace and hope although canonists are not willing to co-
operate in any way to give it the status of a sacrament.

The *ministerial priesthood* of the Church is an efficacious sign of hope to the extent that the priests are assimi-
lated to Christ who is at the same time the High Priest
who gives himself as ransom for his people and the
Prophet who rejects any idle status quo. Christ detested
ritualism, formalism and everything that stifled trust in
God, a longing and striving toward greater union with
God and the realization of man's brotherhood.

Christ is the great sign of hope particularly by his perfect synthesis of love of God with love of neighbor. He
listens to the Father while attending to the needs and
prayers of his people; he proclaims forgiveness of sins
and eternal life while taking care of the diseased and the
hungry. He is the hope of all since he did not come to be

served but to serve. A priest is a visible sign of hope if, not only with words and sacramental rites but also by his life and his relationship to the people, he makes Christ visible, the great sign of hope for all. He makes visible God's gracious presence if he is not so much a "specialist in religion" an expert on rubrics and laws, as a graced and gracious servant of the economy of salvation. The present unrest relative to the understanding of the priesthood and the search for new forms and structures is simply a yearning for the ministerial priesthood to be more visibly a sign of hope for the men of today. All want a hope that transcends all earthly hopes but which, to some extent, incarnates the hopes of daily life as Christ's priesthood was related to the joys and hopes of men.

Celibacy for the heavenly kingdom is not a sacrament in the technical sense but it is a great sign of hope if freely chosen or accepted in faith. When without human planning divine Providence leads to celibacy, if it is lived in joyful expectation for the coming of the Savior and in vigilance for the needs of others, there is a witness to the total vocation and hope of man in Christ.

Illness and the expectation of death are tempting moments; many hopes seem to collapse in the gravely ill. Suffering can disturb and frustrate the mind. Through the sacrament of the *anointing of the sick*, Christ encounters the sick and his family, informing them that all suffering is redeemed, and plays a role in the redemption of mankind when it is united with his death and resurrection. Those who entrust themselves in their illness to Christ and who embrace death as a salvific event number among the most valuable signs and testimonies of the total hope to which Christ calls us.

There are many other situations in life when God bestows on us many precious signs of grace. A "sacramental spirituality"[2] is not limited to these seven sacraments; however, the seven do open all the horizons, give the right perspective, make people aware of God's presence in daily situations and the great moments of life. God, through the Christian witness of persons who are truly "sacraments," makes his people more aware of his presence and his goodness.

[2] Bernard Häring, *A Sacramental Spirituality* (New York: Sheed & Ward, 1965).

9

THE JOYFUL CHARACTER OF HOPE

The Christian religion is not just a system of ethics or a series of commandments; neither can it be restricted to a *commandment* of love. The religious faith of a Christian consists in life with Christ, the fulfilled promise and the final promise of fulfillment.

The impact of Karl Marx's ideology came from its promise of a better world. We are entitled to ask: Why is it that Communism's thrust is now dying if not dead? Personally, I think Communism as an ideology died four years ago in Prague; at least for Czechoslovakia and the greater part of Eastern Europe, it has faded away because of its failure to keep any of its major promises and its pledges for the future are untrustworthy.

In historical retrospect the short-lived influence of Communist hope can be accounted for in religious terms. When Marx began his career, religious doctrine for too many Christians consisted mainly of a catalogue of commandments. Catholics regarded minor man-made fast-and-abstinence laws and the eucharist as equally important. Meatless Fridays were enjoyed with as much rigor as Sunday mass, and the latter had become chiefly a legal ordinance. For many, commitment to work for a more fraternal world was either an unknown or irrelevant Christian notion. In short, religion had degenerated into concern about saving one's own soul and maintenance of the status quo in society. Such was the social and religious setting in which the poor eked out a meager existence.

When Karl Marx proposed his ideas, wrong as they were, they offered a mighty hope, a promise of better things to come. Even the suffering of the oppressed proletariat was regarded by him as a positive factor leading to the final explosion of hatred in the form of revolution and the establishment of eventual brotherhood in a classless society. His whole theory of hope was rooted in the idea that aggression would open doors to a future of everlasting peace.

Many other worldly messianisms are being proposed in this day and age and they will likely exert their seductive influence on people unless Christianity becomes what it should be according to the will of Christ: the greatest of all promises. "The world belongs to whoever offers it the greater hope." From beginning to end, the Christian religion is one of promise, hope and fidelity. It should be enlightening for all to see how the Christians of apostolic times looked upon Christ's life, death and the proclamation of his joyful message.

The first synthesis of apostolic catechesis is found in the Gospel of Mark; it summarizes Christ's whole life, being and preaching. "Christ began to proclaim the gladdening news coming from God. The time of favor has come, the kingdom of God is upon you; be renewed in your mind and believe in the Gospel" (Mk. 1:14–15). Be renewed in your mind by putting your trust in the gladdening news; this is the gist of the message, the full scope of this very short synthesis.

As divine Messenger living in close proximity to the

people, Christ proclaims the good news and does so with
authority. He has come to gladden the hearts and minds
of people. "The time of favor" refers to promises made
earlier; had not the prophets spoken of that time when
the Messenger of peace would proclaim the gladdening
news? Christ begins his mission by preaching in the
synagogue at Nazareth; he reads the scroll: "The spirit of
the Lord is upon me because the Lord has anointed me;
he has sent me to bring good news to the humble" (Lk.
4:18). He is the fulfillment of the prophecies; the promises
of the Old Testament are now fulfilled in him for he has
come to bring joy, peace and hope.

Whatever Christ is and does serves as a preparation
for the resurrection; it is a message of joy and an over-
ture to happiness. Christ does not indulge in a sterile
moralism or bare law because the law can never bring
the fullness of life. Furthermore, if the law has forfeited
its real liberating power, if it becomes a dead law, this
is due to our selfish self. Faith in the good tidings and
trust in Christ who is the gladdening news spell the difference between Christ's teaching and mere moralism. In
summary, Christ proclaims the gladdening message in his
person, in his word and finally in his death and resurrection. For this the Spirit has anointed and sent him;
he in turn sends the Spirit in whom we can joyously cry
out "Abba, Father." The essence of Christian morality
is then a renewal of heart and mind by putting our faith
and trust in the Gospel, in the good tidings. Christ's message is one of hope but hope in the full existential meaning of entrusting ourselves to Christ, our peace and our
Gospel, who is most desirous that we in turn become messengers of joy.

The Sermon on the Mount as recorded in St. Matthew
served as apostolic catechesis in preparation for the sacraments of initiation, i.e., baptism, confirmation and the

eucharist. The evangelist emphasizes the fact that Christ communicates his beatitudes, his message of joy and rule of life in the presence of the crowd; it is not intended just for a few. Surrounded by his disciples, Jesus opens his mouth and delivers the following message: "How blest are those . . ." nine times repeated (Mt. 5:1–7). He communicates his own joy, his own beatitude, his own love, mercy and gentleness. By his whole being and, as pointed out by the Church Fathers, by the mission of the Holy Spirit, he truly gathers all his disciples on the mount of the beatitudes. He communicates to true believers his joy and the blessedness of the Paschal Mystery. The Servant of God and of men who is also the Truth of salvation, the Way and the Life, is the bearer of joy and the source of joy. His joyous message by far takes precedence over the commandments; indeed, the commandments have no meaning for those who do not recognize him as the source of joy, peace and hope.

In Luke's Sermon on the Plain, it is reported that people came to Jesus from Jerusalem, Judea, Samaria and from the heathen cities because power went out from him, an attractive and healing power (Lk. 6:17–19). He then communicated joy but with a clear understanding that those who do not accept him as its source or who do not open themselves to his message of joy and consequently do not follow him on this road are passing judgment on themselves. Woe to them! Without him, there is no joy and no hope; he is the Messenger of joy, hope and peace.

Before presenting the great commandment, the all-embracing directive to "love one another as I have loved you" (Jn. 15:12), Jesus says: "All this I have spoken to you that my joy may be in you and your joy may be complete" (Jn. 15:11). Only those who open themselves to his message of joy, who treasure it up in their hearts,

can bear fruit for the life of the world: "If you dwell in
me and my words dwell in you, ask what you will, and
you shall have it. This is my Father's glory, that you
may bear fruit in plenty and so be my disciples" (Jn.
15:7–8). Only if, like Mary (Lk. 2:19), we cherish in our
hearts the saving message, the gladdening word, only if
it truly dwells in our hearts to be pondered over, will we
bear fruit in love. His Word, which is love and joy, desires
to dwell in us so that we can communicate his life and
joy to the world.

The whole teaching of the Gospel, the preaching of the
apostles and the letters of St. Paul make clear that we will
be sterile and our life will be barren if we close ourselves
to the message of joy. Moralism can be the most hopeless
business in the world if we begin by imposing a commandment instead of first communicating joy. I feel that
the Super-Skunk has done a very effective job in many
parts of the world with bare injunctions, prescriptions,
prohibitions, do's and don'ts; his effectiveness has resulted
in the absolute joylessness and noticeable sterility of
much of Christian life.

In his high priestly prayer, Jesus says: "While I am still
in the world, I speak these words so that they may have
joy within them in full measure" (Jn. 17:13). The purpose
of his coming was to bring us his joy in fullness. If we
cherish his words, his expressions of joy, the communication of his beatitude, and if we agree to follow him who
paved the way for us in the Paschal Mystery, we will
then know the full measure of his joy and will bear the
fruit for which Christ prayed: unity, or oneness, made
possible by putting to death our selfish desires. It is not
possible for man to conquer his selfishness unless he trusts
in Christ and believes in the gladdening news of Christ.

The Gospels clearly indicate that the earliest efforts of
the apostolic communities to synthesize Christ's life and

message depict him as the Messenger of joy and the call to faith. For us, this means a joyous acceptance and treasuring up of his words, allowing them to dwell in us so that they will take on the dynamism which will eventually manifest itself in bearing the fruits of love, joy and peace for the life of the world. Christ's "command" is a word of joy and of grace, communicating his own love and joy.

At all times St. Paul appears as a messenger of joy, preaching incessantly Christ's message of joy. In spite of his many frustrating experiences and captivity, Paul writes to the Philippians: "Yes, and rejoice I will, knowing well that the issue of it all will be my deliverance, because you are praying for me and the Spirit of Jesus Christ is given me for support" (Phil. 1:19). So it is not only in spite of trials but even because of them and the sufferings uniting him to the Paschal Mystery that Paul can say "yes" and rejoice, for he knows well that the issue of all his trials will be his deliverance because "you are praying for me and the Spirit of Jesus Christ is given me for support. For, as I passionately hope, I shall have no cause to be ashamed, but shall speak so boldly that now as always the greatness of Christ will shine out clearly in my person, whether through my life or through my death" (Phil. 1:19–20). The greatness of Christ shines through in both life and death. "For to me life is Christ and death gain" (Phil. 1:21). "Only let your conduct be worthy of the Gospel of Jesus Christ" (Phil. 1:27). The word "Gospel" means the effective communication of joy and hope.

Paul's whole life becomes an encouragement and a source of hope to the early Christians; he rejoices while in jail, while being flogged and while being despised because he knows that in all his trials, the Paschal Mystery is working salvation for him and through him. But for his

beloved disciples and for himself personally, the condition is that their life and conduct be worthy of the gladdening news of the Gospel of Christ. Thus with Christ
he can face death in hope. Christ made death the great
sign of trust: "But if my life blood is to crown that
sacrifice which is the offering up of your faith, I am glad
of it and I share my gladness with you all. Rejoice, you no
less than I, and let us share our joy" (Phil. 2:17–18). It
is while in captivity and while suffering injustice that Paul
preaches this message of peace and joy. Similarly, St.
Ignatius of Antioch, while being "chained to seven leop-
ards" and expecting to be thrown to the lions, sends a
message of joy to Rome: he comes to sacrifice his life
and they should not hinder him; for the believers, there
is reason to rejoice in martyrdom. Such is the strength
of faith in the Paschal Mystery.

Three times Paul attempts to bring to a close and sign
off his Epistle to the Philippians; each time, it is with "I
wish you joy in the Lord." The third time, he repeats: "I
wish you all joy in the Lord. I will say it again: all joy be
yours" (Phil. 4:4).

In the Epistle to the Galatians, when he sets down
the basic rules or criteria for the discernment of genuine
love from its counterfeits, he assigns the first place to love
and posits joy and peace as immediate manifestations of
it (Gal. 5:22). Then follow those attitudes indicative of
peace: patience, kindness, goodness, gentleness and self-
control. These are the signs, the criteria we must observe
if we want to know what applies in our times, whom we
should follow and from whom we should learn. These
attitudes are conspicuously absent in angry, bitter people and in institutional critics whether they be theologians, canonists, bishops, superiors or infallible young or
old people.

At the end of one of his terms in the jails of South

Africa, Gandhi sent a word of peace, a message of goodness to General Jan Christian Smuts who had unjustly imprisoned him. While in prison, he had made a pair of sandals for him. Gandhi informed him that he would continue his non-violent action against suppression and racial discrimination; however, he would do so, convinced that on the other side there are people capable, ultimately, of accepting the message of peace. When in India he started to work out his theology of non-violent action and to gather a group of leaders about him, he began by opening an *ashram,* or house of prayer, a worthy legacy for all of us. Only if we are united with God will he preserve peace and will our actions promote peace in the world.

It matters very little in these times of polarization whether one calls himself a liberal or a conservative; what truly matters is whether or not we number ourselves among the frustrated, bitter and angry people or align ourselves with the peaceful, kind, hopeful and joyful people of God. After listening for more than an hour to a class of deacons verbalizing their dissatisfaction, I finally spoke out: "You are all just reactionaries; you have not offered one constructive comment nor uttered a peaceful word; you are only pitting yourselves against reactionaries." There is a definite danger that criticism will become bitter and frustrated; when this happens, nothing more can be learned. Of course, those who first caused the frustration should not then counter reactionary criticism with more bitter criticism. It is then time for everybody to come to his senses, to give in and pray for peace. The criterion in this case should not be so much readiness to change as the basic Christian attitude of joy and peace. It should then be possible to see the direction which change should take. So once again, we are faced with the fundamental question: Where do we get this joy and peace?

The answer can be found in the theology of shalom in the Old Testament; it is God's undeserved gift. It can only be received through humble prayer, in a spirit of gratitude, and it can only remain with those who are ready to promote peace. Christian hope does not emanate from man's heart or mind. However, there is already an investment of hope on earth; all that is good, right, just, honest and beautiful from the past represents man's co-operation with and response to God's undeserved gift. He has given us his promises and we should open-mindedly look about and try to find Christ in all things, for all things are made by him and for him.

Finally, it is Christ himself we are seeking, the fullness of peace and joy. But the initiative is God's and this point is paramount in a theology of hope. We will always experience frustration and tensions if we rely solely on our own initiative. Nevertheless, we have to acknowledge man's special way of honoring God's graciousness; man will be creative, spontaneous and generous, but the basis of man's creativity lies in his awareness of God's initiative, and his joy will then stem from his loving response to God's loving advances.

10

HOPE AND RESPONSIBILITY
FOR THE WORLD

God has never left man without hope. However the genuine, all-embracing character of hope, the gift of the one Father of all, has often been obscured by various side streams of religious thought. This is true within Christianity and even more so outside of it. One instance would be hope as understood by Hinayana, or "small boat," Buddhism where it meant escaping the wheel of life by withdrawal from society. The Buddhists of this school renounced the desires and promises of this world and longed for nirvana, i.e., the final beatitude attained through the extinction of all desires. Buddhist monks and nuns of the Hinayana were highly individualistic; they wanted to save themselves personally on the small boat of the negation of life. A turn in the history of Buddhism introduces the Bodhisattva, a being that compassionately refrains from entering nirvana in order to save others. This form of Buddhism can be looked upon as somehow foreshadowing salvation in Christ.

According to Buddhist lore, the Bodhisattva first embarked on the small boat of salvation, renouncing all the desires of life and did so in perfect sincerity. However, when he arrived at the doors of nirvana and stood there about to enter, he realized that he was confronting the fullness of life, community and love. Mindful of this he bids God not to let him enter but rather to send him back to his brethren to bring them the message that life is not mere negation; life is actually fullness in brotherhood. So he embarked on the big boat (*Mahayana* Buddhism), which connotes concern for the salvation of all. This Buddhist hymn foreshadows Christ in a way very similar to the poems of Isaiah (Chs. 40 ff.). In the Bodhisattva we can detect the finger of God singling out and sending religious men to open up horizons of hope.

Within every religion we find people tempted to escape from the heat of the day and the turmoils of life; they want to save their souls "on the small boat" and embark on a course of religious individualism. Even Christianity has known similar side streams contaminating the disciples of Christ such as Manichaeism, Gnosticism and Parsiism. Each of these cults was marked by a quest for self-fulfillment or an individualistic personalism incapable of leading to the fullness of life. Complete self-realization comes only through openness to the totality of God's work and an authentic faith in the Savior of the world.

Christ fulfilled Deutero-Isaiah's prophecy about the Servant Messiah. Christ neither eludes his brethren nor shuns their problems; on the contrary, he comes for them as the Word Incarnate. He lives a common life and shares the burden of all mankind; he bears the heat of the day until death. He is not a Savior of disincarnate souls as the Gnostics would have it; he is the Savior of the world, of man in his wholeness and man in his world. His message is other-worldly, freeing man from this-worldly pride and worry but sending him into this world as messenger of peace and justice. He proclaims a new way of life which is beyond the sinful world, but there is no way to reach out for eternal life except through love of men. The big boat on which he embarks with his disciples is that of service to the hungry, the needy, the blind, the lame and the imprisoned. His Sermon on the Mount calls for brotherliness in the world and the spirit of the poor, that is, acknowledgment that all God's gifts come from the Father and therefore serve as an appeal for us to share with everybody including our enemies. If the initial call to faith reminds us of what is most precious, salvation for eternal life, it must logically become a saving sign for this world. Those who have committed themselves to the hope of everlasting life must work to strengthen all worthy earthly hopes: hope of justice, goodness, mercy, peace, brotherhood and so on.

Apart from Christ, the Christian cannot embark on the "big boat," the saving boat of hope for the present and the world to come. The reality of salvation rests in the promise of Christ who reveals the Father to us. To know him and the Father and through him to know how the Father loves the world is salvation for whoever knows him and unites himself to him for loving service of the brethren. Christ lives and dies for the glory of his Father, but he translates his devotion by a passionate concern for man and his world. Christ came to manifest the full extent and full depth of the Father's love for the created universe. His obedience to the Father's design makes him the bread of life for the world; he even offers his body and blood for it. The incarnation, death and resurrection of Christ constitute the greatest investment of hope ever known and manifest the nearness of the Emmanuel to his human brethren. Christ remains particularly close to those for whom the proud and self-righteous world offers little hope.

When the Christian sets sail on the big boat of brotherhood in this world, he sets out for new horizons, eternal

life in the community of saints and the concelebration of
God's triune love. He realizes that it is only on the big
boat of solidarity with Christ that he can attain his goal
because he believes in Christ, the Savior of man who is
concerned for him and his world.

Christ's mission embraces the whole created universe,
the entire world in which man lives. He is the life and
light of the world: "God loved the world so much that he
gave his only Son. . . . It was not to judge the world
that God sent his Son into the world, but that through
him the world might be saved" (Jn. 3:16–17). Only in
very specific contexts of the New Testament is the word
"world" used in a pejorative sense, as in the Gospel of
John where Jesus says, "I am not praying for the world
but for those whom thou hast given me" (Jn. 17:9); here
it is a *sacred* world that has become godless instead of
opening itself to the saving solidarity and unity in Christ.
The "godless world" of the Gospel of John refers to those
men of the religious Establishment who built up their
comfortable nook of limited religious concern and who
even used "religion" instrumentally for their career, their
own pride, vanity and power. This same danger arises
again and again. We could designate as "unholy worldli-
ness" that which the Bible called "godless world." Such
people are also unconcerned for the poor and are oblivious of the prophetic tradition related to concern for
orphans, widows, aliens or strangers. They form an arti-
ficial and godless world of their own because they do not
share God's love for the real world.

The whole universe called into being by the creative
Word senses somehow the presence of the saving Word.
Hence citizens of the frustrated world still yearn and
groan inwardly for hope in saving solidarity. All who are
trained by vanity or affected by the domineering attitude
of old "Adam and Eve," all who suffer in the pernicious

solidarity of oppressive power structures, implicitly bid the disciples of Christ to relieve their misery by bringing them a share in the freedom of the sons and daughters of God. They long for "salvation" while crying out for a more just and more humane world. Without yet knowing Christ as the Giver of everlasting life, they express their hope in him through their desire for justice not only for themselves but for the whole world. Those who are visibly on the way to greater liberation from selfish individualism and group egotism, who are sailing on the big boat of salvation for all, are truly signs of hope for the world. Their concern for man in his daily needs and their peaceful struggle for a healthier world can open the eyes of all men of good will to the greater hope of eternal life. Their solicitude becomes all the more convincing because this very hope inspires commitment to a better world.

St. Paul develops the same theme in his own way: "There is no condemnation for those who are united with Christ Jesus, because in Christ Jesus the life-giving law of the Spirit has set you free from the law of sin and death. What the law could never do because our selfish self robbed it of all potency, God has done: by sending his own Son in a form like that of our sinful nature, and as a sacrifice for sin, he has passed judgment against sin within that very nature, so that the commandment of the law may find fulfillment in us, whose conduct, no longer under the control of our lower nature, is directed by the Spirit" (Rom. 8:1–4). Paul also stresses the existential viewpoint; man must dedicate himself to hope by opening himself to the new perspective which is the absolute condition for becoming a sign of hope for the world. "Those who live on the level of the selfish nature have their outlook formed by it, and that spells death; but those who live on the level of the Spirit have the spiritual outlook, and that is life and peace. For the outlook of the selfish is enmity with God; it is not subject to the law of God; indeed it cannot be; those who live on such a level cannot possibly please God" (Rom. 8:5-8).

Paul trusts that God's grace will set free the true self in man and conquer selfishness: "But that is not how you live. You are on the spiritual level, if only God's Spirit dwells within you; and if a man does not possess the Spirit of Christ, he is no Christian. But if Christ is dwelling within you, then although the body is a dead thing because you sinned, yet the spirit is life itself because you have been justified. Moreover, if the Spirit of Him who raised Jesus from the dead dwells within you, then the God who raised Christ Jesus from the dead will also give new life to your mortal bodies through his indwelling Spirit" (Rom. 8:9-11). The new outlook that initiates saving relationships already manifests its saving power here on earth and thus strengthens the hope of resurrection. Gospel freedom through docility to the Spirit is also Gospel solidarity of the sons of God in Christ.

"For all who are moved by the Spirit of God are sons of God. The Spirit you have received is not a spirit of slavery leading you back into a life of fear, but a Spirit that makes us sons, enabling us to cry 'Abba, Father!' In that cry the Spirit of God joins with our spirit in testifying that we are God's children; and if children, then heirs. We are God's heirs and Christ's fellow-heirs, if we share his sufferings now in order to share his splendor hereafter" (Rom. 8:14-17). Through the gift of the Spirit, the necessity to suffer in this world is no longer merely a frustrated sharing but a redeeming and saving one for the life of the world. Christ's suffering brings hope to the whole world in all and through all who, under the law of grace, dedicate themselves for the salvation of the world.

The liberating power of solidarity in Christ through

his Spirit opens up new horizons for temporal hope, but they are not restricted to the temporal and this-worldly hopes; they are synchronized or integrated into the greater vision of Christian hope. "For I reckon that the sufferings we now endure bear no comparison with the splendor, as yet unrevealed, which is in store for us. For the created universe waits with eager expectation for God's sons to be revealed. It was made the victim of frustration, not by its own choice, but because of him who made it so" (Rom. 8:18–20). This text can be translated and explained in a number of different ways: the "who made it so" can be Adam, the sinner, and the collectivity of sinners, the "collective Adam" who subjects the created universe to frustration. It can also be explained in the following way, and I think this is the right explanation: God created everything with a view of solidarity and if man opts for a selfish, sinful and frustrating outlook on life, then by necessity he contaminates the world about him; he becomes a center of frustration for the world because God has created everything for solidarity. If by his life man does not cry "Abba, Father!" in brotherhood, then by necessity he is radiating frustration about him. "Yet always there was hope, because the universe itself is to be freed from the shackles of mortality and enter upon the liberty and splendor of the children of God" (Rom. 8:21). If sin has a cosmic dimension, all the more does salvation embrace the whole universe. We can expect to find evidence of kindness, joy, hope, goodness, peace and reconciliation in the world around the true children of God. This is the vision proposed by Paul's Gospel of hope. It is not that other-worldliness of alienation of which Karl Marx accused the selfish and individualistic Christians. According to Paul, the outcry of adoration, the Magnificat for God's grace means dedication as in the case of Mary, the handmaid, who remained forever vigilant for the needs of people.

"Up to the present, we know, the whole created universe groans in all its parts as if in the pangs of childbirth" (Rom. 8:22). Today particularly we can understand the meaning of Paul's text; the secular world and the Church herself, including many religious congregations, are still moaning with labor pains. Since only hope imparts meaning to the pangs of childbirth, those who yield to pessimism and waste time in futile lamentations are really aborting the child. Christ-like hope is tested by tensions, conflicts and suffering. On the contrary, those who agree to pay the price for joy in hope are actually pioneering a new age. Salvation is operative in that hope because it is marked by the Paschal Mystery. Christ frees us from the illusions of individualistic hope. Growing pains become signs of hope when believers succeed in synthesizing renewal, understood as personal conversion, and a common effort for building a better milieu. Salvation becomes visible in that community of faith and hope which cares effectively for a healthier world in which to live. The created universe, the whole world around us, is frustrated by all the various conflicting structures and superstructures of selfishness, power and individualism. It groans and yearns for God's wisdom to manifest itself more powerfully. The redeemed want the new age of redemption to prevail in the history of mankind and thus to witness to hope in everlasting life. Salvation cannot be divorced from responsibility to the world. Our hopes are bound up with the destiny of the world in which we live.

The outcry of the created universe can serve our best interests and we should listen to it if we want to live in hope. "Not only so, but even we, to whom the Spirit is given as first fruits of the harvest to come, are groaning inwardly while we wait for God to make us his sons and set our whole body free. For we have been saved, though only in hope. Now to see is no longer to hope: why should a man endure and wait for what he already sees? But if we hope for something we do not see, then, in waiting for it, we show our endurance" (Rom. 8:23–25).

Salvation through the process of hope begets endurance in solidarity. Those who have come to appreciate fully how they have been saved by hope take upon themselves the burdens of their communities as well as the tradition and burden of the Church. However, this is only possible by paying hope-filled attention to the goodness, truth and example of the saints which is nothing less than an investment of Christ's redemptive love in the world. Only with hope and gratitude can we assume the burdens of the so-called "Old World" in the Church and overcome its debilitating effects. The Church will then realize better her own solidarity with the whole world. One of the great themes of today's theology has become: how to relate the world to come, everlasting life, our hope of seeing God face to face, with present reality and with our actual joys, fears and hopes.

Christian hope is a talent or a gift of God entrusted to his disciples, an investment for the reconciliation of the world around them, the world in which they live. The talent is committed to their care so that they may become signs of hope for the world. Without gratitude, however, the gift can be lost. Gratefulness expresses itself when the talent is used to generate any kind of positive element of hope for our world, for God's world. Gratitude for both the promise and the gift we have received means active hope, i.e., hope-at-work taking advantage of all real opportunities to save the world, recognizing them as such and responding to the *kairos*, the time of favor or present opportunities. Hope and gratitude enable us to respond to the yearning of the world around us, to have a share in the first fruits of the free sons and daughters of God and to be freed from selfishness and narrowness. Thus Christian life means commitment to and celebration of gratitude in hope, a celebration before God and in one's daily work.

We can equally well say that Christian life means celebration of hope in gratitude and celebration of gratitude in hope. It always implies a commitment to the world around us. The Christian celebration of gratitude and hope is impossible without an active commitment to redemption in response to the groaning of the world, that is, the desires of the world to have a share in the freedom of the sons and daughters of God.

The Christian has placed his hope in the one God, the one Father, the one Creator of all things, and in the one Redeemer of the world who gives himself as the bread "for the life of the world" (Jn. 6:51). He has hope, faith and trust in the one Spirit who renews the face of the earth. The Christian sees the opposing powers of darkness but the believer knows in faith that the dark powers will not prevail; however, he will be on the side of the victor only if he bears the burden, the heat of the day, according to the measure of the gifts he has received. What we are hoping for is the community of saints, the perfect brotherhood in the new earth and the new heaven. This hope inspires and quickens meaningful solidarity with all men and all creatures: political, social, economic, cultural and every kind of solidarity. If we one day discover other personal creatures on other planets, we must seek solidarity with them because they too are made by God's Word and for Christ.

Christian hope does not look for beatitude of a romantic I-Thou type but is a sharing or concelebration of God's redeeming and gladdening love. Life is a pilgrim situation; only through faithful solidarity with the expectations of all men and all creatures can we be on the way to final sharing and concelebration. Although we are sinners, we have hope because of the gladdening news of reconciliation. We hope for the fullness of joy and peace. Therefore true believers will make a constant investment of hope, optimism, forgiveness, peace and reconciliation out of a sense of responsibility for God's world. The hope and joy, love and faith in the gladdening news must be incarnate on the soil of human history since it is proclaimed by the Word Incarnate who lived the common life of people while expressing a saving concern for all men around him.

The Pharisees and priests who did not believe in a servant Messiah wanted pure signs of power. The signs which Christ gives, on the contrary, are expressions of a healing love and a testimony of responsibility for the real needs of people. They satisfy man's temporal hopes by awakening hope for final salvation.

We hope for the new earth and the new heaven. We know that in the final analysis, only God's radiating and transforming power will bring us this new earth and new heaven. However in the Word Incarnate who calls us to be sharers of his redeeming love for the world, God calls us to renew the earth by making a new investment in hope, justice, goodness, mercy and peace. Consequently, our hope cannot be genuine unless we actively express our faith that in the incarnation of God's Word the redemption of the earth has already begun. This is a seed entrusted to those who know that they are saved by a hope corresponding to the yearning of the world to be freed from the slavery of sin. The dogma of the incarnation does not allow us to be content with a lazy apocalyptic hope, waiting as it were in a watchtower of dreams for the day and hour of the Lord's coming and thus escaping from any daily reponsibilities. Eschatological hope in the biblical sense means a dynamic hope and active commitment to the world here and now in view of the final hope.

The messianic peace is an undeserved gift and equally undeserved promise of the final fullness of peace and joy. But only those persons accept and honor this gift who commit themselves here and now to the order of peace. The unselfishness, purity of intention and energy of hope with which believers commit themselves to peace on earth, to justice and human development, and to the unity and solidarity of all men, is the best indication of and witness for the full scope of the messianic peace.

We should not overlook the fact, however, that there can be genuine responsibility for the world inspired by a firm hope for human history alone, a hope manifesting itself in solidarity and justice without any explicit hope of eternal life. The patriarchs of Israel probably had great hope of future peace on earth before they came to a full vision of eternal life and the resurrection of the individual person. But as their trust in God, their experience with his covenant and their feeling of a call to solidarity in the covenant grew, their hopes were projected to horizons beyond Israel and beyond this earthly life.

Talk about "anonymous Christians" can give the impression that those who do not know Christ have generally a Christ-like love. But everyone can see that such is not the case. When confronted with Christ's saving love, so much of what the world calls "love" is unmasked as a lie. The same holds true of many forms of temporal hope.

There are forms of hope which betray man's pride, his foolish trust in himself, in technical progress, power and so on. The hope God offers in his covenant to man is often built on the breakdown of such arrogant hopes. Neverthe-

less, as I have indicated earlier, there are genuine forms
of temporal hope such as a commitment to peace, dedication to racial reconciliation and social justice; it is the
hope that the dignity of each person will be respected.
This kind of hope is a precious talent entrusted by God
to man. Wherever this talent is put to good use through
God's presence, mankind comes closer to God's promises
for this age and for the world to come.

Human hope, trust, optimism and perseverance in the
commitment to a better future can reflect the fullness of
eschatological hope. They can have the quality of an
analogia spei, that is, a hidden presence, an initial manifestation of ever greater hope, a reality longing for an
ever greater God and pointing to trust in him. Whatever
is good and right in temporal hope, in mutual trust and
dedication to the future of others, is already quickened
by the same God who gives the fullness of his promises
in Jesus Christ. As long as man transcends himself and
opens himself to the common future of all in hope, we
have hopeful degrees of consciousness pointing toward
that hope in Christ in which all the dimensions of man's
calling come into play.

We need to look at the whole experience of temporal
hope in order to get a vital picture of the hope to which
Christ calls us. For instance, we notice that in difficult
situations strong men tend to fade away as soon as they
have given up hope. On the other hand, we know how
weak bodies reacted to similarly trying situations in jail
and in prison camps because these persons did not abandon hope for a single moment; very often their hope was
sustained by the trust shown them by beloved persons.
We know how a difficult or seemingly ungifted child can
be helped to develop if he is shown trust and given credit
in a convincing way. On the other hand, if a doctor,
analyst or confessor informs a neurotic person that he

even lacks the freedom to commit a venial sin, he destroys all hope and thwarts all efforts which could have been inspired by more patient encouragement and understanding.

We know from our experience with human hope in daily life that a person cannot preserve and strengthen his hope without making an appropriate effort to obtain the things hoped for. By a persistent and prudent effort to obtain worthwhile things with a firm attitude of hope, we prepare people for a better understanding of the dynamism of Christian hope.

Our dynamic culture today provides daily proof that those who become self-complacent, whether in economic or professional life or in politics, are headed for failure and pessimism. We should accept this as a warning against any static perspective with respect to Christian life and hope. Hope lives and grows when the whole life of the Church and of the person is seen as a constant process of renewal, as a continuous conversion and a tireless striving. Hope exists when the pilgrim Church and each individual person knows and is fully aware that on earth love can never be perfect but needs forever to grow in response to God's call: "Be all goodness just as your heavenly Father is all good" (Mt. 5:48). The realization that all human achievements are unfinished tasks can serve as a strong impetus to a vital understanding of Christian hope.

Partial failures are the lot of man; they can even arouse him to exert new energies provided man does not give up hope. Experience here sheds light on an important aspect of the Gospel of reconciliation. The sinner turning more decidedly toward God and awakening to greater vigilance and unceasing prayer realizes that God can write straight on crooked lines.

Quite often acceptance of one's responsibilities in the

temporal realm can entail disquiet, conflict and contradiction. However, men of hope mature in the most difficult moments of life. If these experiences are seen in the light of faith, we realize better that suffering and conflict accepted in Christ can lead to perseverance and render hope more stable.

11
THE HUMAN BODY
AS AN EXPRESSION OF HOPE

The firm conviction of the Greek philosophers concerning the immortality of the human spirit facilitated the diffusion of the Christian message of salvation and the promise of eternal life throughout the Hellenistic world. Their point of departure came from the daily experience of the body's impending death and final dissolution. But even in the course of man's physical life, the spiritual principle manifests itself within a mortal body. Is it not also dissolved in death like the body?

Greek philosophy, which corresponded to the mentality of the people, responded decisively in the negative. It contended that only death can properly and fully set free the spirit. This conviction evidently expresses a great hope. But the body is not necessarily excluded and we are not allowed to arrive at such a conclusion. Since the body serves as a bridge with the visible physical world, therefrom stems its value. Why should the soul, which definitively finds refuge from this visible world in an invisible one, ever commit itself so fundamentally for that which, after all, constitutes only a temporary prison? Such a preoccupation for the soul became one of the reasons behind a certain disinterest of religion in the problems of every-day life.

On the other hand, the biblical message views the body, and consequently, the visible world, in the full light of hope. God is the Creator and the Redeemer not only of invisible souls but also of the visible universe in its total-ity. Just as sin and its deleterious solidarity are inscribed in human existence and in the visible environment of man, so redemption assumes the task and addresses itself to the challenges of the body and of the universe. The doctrine of creation regards the human body or, better, the totality of man in his physical manifestation, as a masterpiece of God. The closer man gets to God's crea-tive design, the more his likeness to God shines through in his body.

Unlike the Greeks, the just of the Old Testament finds no solace for death in the natural immortality of the soul. His one consolation is an unlimited trust in God even if he fails to see very clearly how God's goodness will be expressed toward him personally after his death. In a Hebraic culture that attributed an all-important place to the body, this limitless faith in the God of prom-ises develops gradually and slowly, according to the plan of Divine Providence, in the firm hope that the body would not be forever doomed to hell. Even before the coming of Christ, hope in the resurrection of the body already constituted a central argument among the pious Israelites.

Christ, the Word of the Father made man, has re-deemed us through his corporeal death and in his resur-rection; he has given us the pledge of all our hope, has brought the aforementioned evolution of the hope of Israel to full circle and to the security of faith. The primitive Church committed itself to this vital core of hope with the full force of its faith. It admitted no evasion into the speculative world of invisible spirits which in some way or other would cloud the integral hope granted by Christ's incarnation and resurrection. The Epistle to the Colossians constitutes an eloquent testimony to this attitude. The First Letter of John aligns the Gnostics with the "impious world." They tended to depreciate the material-visible world and addressed themselves completely to that of the angels, of immortal spirits and ideas. They consequently evinced skepticism about the Incarnation of Christ and the resurrection of the body.

Hope in the resurrection, and therefore, in the eternal life of the whole man constitutes a sign of hope for the world created by God. Faith in the resurrection of Christ and hope in the resurrection of the body is not limited to a decisive blocking of Gnosticism and Manichaeism, but it also establishes the line of demarcation between an admissible Hellenization of the message of Christ and that which is inadmissible: "Now if this is what we proclaim, that Christ was raised from the dead, how can some of you say there is no resurrection of the dead?" (1 Cor. 15:12).

Faith in the resurrection represents the decisive sign of the Christian eluding the world of those who are interested only in spirits, angels and ideas, and others who situate everything in the present world and its progress. That which decided Paul against the Hellenistic tendencies applies equally well against the modern currents which seek their God and their future exclusively in the profane world. "If it is for this life only that Christ has given us hope, we of all men are most to be pitied" (1 Cor. 15:19). This temporal life in the body is a sign of hope, but only through the sign of the cross and of the resurrection of Christ: "The seed you sow does not come to life unless it has first died. . . . What is sown in the earth as a perishable thing is raised imperishable . . . sown as an animal body, it is raised as a spiritual body. If there is such a thing as an animal body, there is also a spiritual body. It is in this sense that Scripture says, 'The first man, Adam, became an animate being,' whereas the last Adam has become a life-giving spirit" (1 Cor. 15:36–45).

The whole of creation hopes on the strength of the resurrection of Christ in his mortal human body. Even pain and death are involved in this hope. "If the Spirit of him who raised Jesus from the dead dwells within you, then the God who raised Christ Jesus from the dead will also give new life to your mortal bodies through his indwelling Spirit" (Rom. 8:11). In final analysis, our hope in eternal life is not founded on the metaphysical principle of the immortality of the spirit, but on the central fact of the history of salvation constituted from the death and resurrection of Christ. It is this truth of faith which obliges us to lead a life in accord with this hope. "It follows, my friends, that our lower nature has no claim upon us; we are not obliged to live on that level. If you do so, you must die. But if by the Spirit you put to death all the base pursuits of the body, then you will live" (Rom. 8:12–13). It is not a question, then, of an *ascesis* inimical to the body or even of a mortification of the corporeal element, but of a life according to the Spirit of Christ and in virtue of the Spirit which has been given, that is to say, a mortification of egotism.

In the perspective of the expected resurrection of the body which sets an orientation and establishes a norm for the whole of our earthly existence, there can also be seen the yearning of the whole of creation. "The universe itself is to be freed from the shackles of mortality and enter upon the liberty and splendor of the children of God. Up to the present, we know, the whole created universe groans in all its parts as if in the pangs of childbirth. Not only so, but even we, to whom the Spirit is given as first fruits of the harvest to come, are groaning inwardly while we wait for God to make us his sons and set our whole body free" (Rom. 8:21–23).

The promises of God became visible as never before in the body of his Son Incarnate. In him, God's goodness and love for man were made corporeally visible. Finally, God's full glory shines forth in the risen body of Christ. But his corporeal life on earth is already a sacrament of hope: his power of attraction, his bodily proximity to all men, the infinite love and supreme surrender which, in the passion and death of Jesus, become visible as the ultimate promise. The love of Christ is not addressed only to souls, for he is the Divine Therapist of the blind, the cripple and the paraplegic. Even when his passion and death attest to the fact that health and terrestrial life are not the essential, his healing action is a distinctive sign of the coming of the reign of God which includes rather specifically the physique of man (cf. Mt. 11:2–6).

In his bodily visibility, in the love made manifest by his corporeality, Christ is "the image of the invisible God" (Col. 1:15; cf. 2 Cor. 4:4). God wants that "in this body also life may reveal itself, the life that Jesus lives" (2 Cor. 4:10) and not only on the day of the resurrection, but in a form already in keeping with our earthly pilgrimage. Trust that Christ "will transfigure the body belonging to our humble state, and give it a form like that of his own resplendent body" (Phil. 3:21) is a law of hope, an effective inducement to "honor God in the body" (1 Cor. 6:20) during our earthly existence.

In all these declarations, there is not even a minimal emphasis on a sacralization of the body in its purely biological aspect. Rather, the question revolves about the holy vocation to translate the love of God in our physical life including the realm of sexual morality. The supreme

act lies in giving one's physical life for others: "There is
no greater love than this, that a man should lay down his
life for his friends" (Jn. 15:13). The motivational picture
includes a high esteem for the body and bodily life. One
can even give his own life to save that of his neighbor,
but the supreme gesture receives its ultimate meaning
from our hope in eternal life.

The grandiose stadium constructed in Rome by Mus-
solini displays a great number of statues of athletes: all
have well-developed muscles and strong taurine necks,
but a small and low forehead crowns an expressionless
face. They were made for wrestling and for war. Con-
trariwise, the great tradition of Christian art portrays the
human body as the image of God, as a real promise of
goodness, compassion and passion for true justice. The
fundamental attitudes of the eschatological man: gratitude, praise, trust, peace and purified passions, vigilance
and joy are inscribed in the human physiognomy. The
spiritual is incarnated while the body is spiritualized. All
this expresses the promise. Even the withered countenance of the grandmother and her trembling hands
folded in prayer become a symbol of hope and a manifestation of maturity for the faithful.

A countenance radiating goodness and cordiality is a
reflection of God's graciousness. The Greek term which
we translate "charis" points exactly to this image. If God
is favorable, he reveals his beaming countenance to us,
he turns his face to man. He often does so with those
men privileged by grace, whose physiognomy and
whole visible bearing are a kind of intimation of the
goodness and graciousness of God.

The hands of a man constitute a marvelous instru-
ment which can serve varied purposes and do many
things, but they can express much more. A hand held out
becomes a sign of reconciliation. A handshake confirms

an alliance or agreement. Hands resting one in the other communicate confidence and trust.

In the four sacred books of Confucius, one can read: "The gifts which heaven has bestowed on the wise man are the fundamental attitudes of benevolence, justice, politeness and prudence. All of these have their roots in the heart. But their effects shine through the face, are revealed in the attitude of the shoulders and in all the members of the body." With the best Chinese tradition, Confucius holds a very particular esteem for politeness, the looking-glass of one's interior life.

A biblical conception of the body in relation to hope cannot make of sexuality an end in itself nor reduce it to the Aristotelian category of "means for reproduction." In the sexual union of man and wife, one comes to know the other intimately. Intentionally or not, spouses manifest even in their sexual behavior that which is rooted in the heart: either an effective gift of self in faithful love or an egotistical use and abuse of the other.

The idea that the human body (including sexuality, which certainly surpasses the purely bodily dimension) has a remote prehistory in the evolution of matter, of the vegetal and animal life, no longer astounds us today. Is not the manner in which the flowers propagate themselves with a marvelous luxuriance in florescence, pollination and fruit-bearing a promise of the generous love of the spouses, the spiritual presupposition and nesting ground in which their children are to be born and raised? It would be sufficient to read, for example, the book of Wolfgang Wickler *Sind wir alle Sünder* (Droemer-Knaur, Munich, 1969) to get an idea to what extent, even in the animal domain, the sexual manifestations surpass the categories of copulation for a reproductive purpose. We find there countless promises which we see fulfilled in the expressions of marital tenderness, in the love play and loving union of the spouses. The moment at which the typically human brain was formed and God breathed into the body a spiritual breath also constituted a promise for sexuality and certainly also a mission never completely fulfilled: it ought to become a conscious and legitimate expression of the spouses' faithful love in the fulfillment of a great vocation.

Human sexuality substantially surpasses that of the animals, even of the most sophisticated and highly evolved mammals and primates. There is no doubt that there is a question here of a qualitative leap. Sexuality in man becomes a language, the expression of an irrevocable gift, a conscious communication in a total communion of life. As a temporal symbolical language, it becomes part of an experience of love which gives and is given to, and which confers irreplaceable energies to Christian faith in the God of love, and hope in the eternal community of love. Sexuality is thus a real symbol of the essential character of matrimony which the Church numbers among its seven sacraments.

Human sexuality is not yet in its pure reality, in its simple existentiality, a sign or a promotion of Christian hope. It never automatically and by itself guarantees definitive fulfillment. And if it attempts to encompass everything, it becomes a source of tragic disillusionment. In its essential relationship to the human person, sexuality is directed to the integration of the total communication network in personal life and in a way such as to contribute to human fulfillment and to hope, but only to the extent that a person truly transcends the self in the sexual rapport with the other, says a "yes" to the "thou" in full availability for the "we" of the familial community.

Like the whole of man, sexuality also has need of redemption. It calls for man to include it in his continuing conversion. If he surrenders himself to egotism, even his sexual behavior will translate his retreat from his ego-ideal and will contribute to a progressive disintegration of the human community. It is therefore evident that sexual disorders demand an integral therapy of the whole human person. If instead of egocentric pursuits, the person and the community behaving likewise live effectively according to Christian hope, such a transforming action will also be manifested in the sexual life.

I am not thinking exclusively or primarily of the transfiguration which human sexuality undergoes in celibacy freely chosen and fully lived for the love of the kingdom of heaven, where simultaneously all the human energies find their redemption and spiritualization in a realization of the love of God for men and for the world without giving way to any forms of hostility for the body. In the celibate, there is no need for any sexual bond with another person; it is a case in which is to be realized an authentic sublimation even of sexual energies. Our reflection on this point is directed rather to sexuality in strong and tender conjugal love, to the rapports linking the partners to an irrevocable fidelity and to their parental vocation. They will experience fully the creative and redemptive love of God if they set for their life and sexual experiences an orientation of hope. In such instances, there is always implied acceptance of the constant limitations in the capacity for an expressive and felicitous sexual encounter, but because of the readiness to experience and to accept limits, sexuality becomes integrated into a married love life and forestalls all idolatry of it.

A unilateral emphasis on the finalistic character of sexuality in view of preservation of the species was understandable in other historical periods. Think only of the constant threat weighing over the human family in earlier times because of the high rate of infant mortality

and epidemics. One need also take into account the bat-
tles waged by the Church against the Gnostic and Mani-
chaean heresies. As opposed to those who, seeking to depreciate the body, considered procreation and generation
as a wrong against a pre-existing soul, there was need to
set in relief the goodness of procreation. But a compli-
cated one-sided emphasis can never serve to complete the
humanization of sexuality. This ought to become a sign of
hope not only for biological fertility but for the fecundity
of love itself.

The Hellenistic culture with its hostility toward the
body, Roman juridicism and Germanic aggressiveness
were not favorable to a full understanding of sexuality.
The conflicting views within the Church ought to be
evaluated in the context of cultural evolution. We should
be astounded by the fact that, in spite of all the contrary
influences, marriage has always been recognized in its
full sacramental dignity as an efficacious sign of salvation,
to remain for always a bond of love rather than of fertility. In the theology of the Oriental Churches, the fact
that human sexuality was never estranged from the grandiose vision of the transfiguration is due to the action of
the Holy Spirit. Gregory of Nazianzus sings, in a hymn
dedicated to his mother on the occasion of her obsequies,
that through her physical love for her husband (who is
the father of the saint) she led him to spiritual unity in
faith and in hope.

In consecrated celibacy as much as in matrimony, sexuality is not more than a promise. The incarnation of
love, whether in conjugal intercourse or in energies nur-
tured by a successful sublimation of sexuality, does not
represent a conclusive work which can be considered
with complacency. The faithful ought not to behave na-
ïvely when confronted by sexuality. It is always a question of the global mission of physical existence and of

its "transfiguration" through a generous love which hopes everything.

Christian hope in all of its dimensions constitutes the best criterion for a theology of sexuality and for a continuous striving of the spouses in view of an ever better integration of their sexual life within the context of their bond of love. Christian hope protects from discouragement those engaged in the struggle and shields them from the idolatry of sexuality. It forbids the exclusion of sexuality from its compass, but neither does it consent to make it the principal object of yearning and of hope.

12
ABOUNDING IN PEACE

Earthly hopes, as long as they remain true to life and open for the ever greater hope, are a gift and sign of the peace that comes from God. All gladdening events in the secular realm, when they strengthen hope and breed open-mindedness, lead finally to Christ since they have in them a final ground for hope. But the ways of experience are many and varied. Some people need a great deal of happy earthly experiences, much encouragement and sometimes a good deal of frustration prior to the collapse of their illusions; they eventually come upon the fountain of all hope, God who in Jesus Christ meets our deepest desires. For others, the full sun of hope rises early; they promptly behold Christ, the Light and Life of the world. Far from being dazzled by his overwhelming brightness, they gradually envision all things and events in the light of Christ. They in turn become reflectors of light and hope; everyone coming in contact with them realizes that such persons do not consider themselves to be the source of light and peace. Their whole existence turns attention to Christ.

It is in this sense that we consider the messianic peace

(shalom), the great gift of Christ in view of a new order of love and hope. Shalom, the unequaled gift of Easter Sunday, becomes light only for the person who truly accepts it as an undeserved favor intended to inundate the world in peace. It is a gift to the individual person but one that presses to become a stream of hope for many.

In Christian hope, we learn that God in Jesus Christ offers peace and salvation to those who entrust themselves to him and accept their mission as messengers of hope for the world. We allow God's Word and gracious gift to become plenitude flowing over into the fullness of peace and knowledge of Jesus Christ which transcends all knowledge (cf. Eph. 3:19). Whoever humbly and gratefully accepts the peace of Christ will realize ever more that Christ is the hope for all of mankind and the whole created universe. Whoever truly lives in faith with Christ, the peace and hope of the world, will come to better understand his own mission as one of co-operation in the redemption of all earthly hopes and in the manifestation of the power of the messianic peace throughout his life.

The overflowing peace of Christ manifests itself abundantly in a life according to the Beatitudes and the evangelical counsels. Those persons who accept the grace of the Holy Spirit and every gift of God as their rule of life will not only show why peacemakers are called the sons and daughters of God (Mt. 5:9) but will cleverly direct the attention of others to the only begotten Son of the Father who has come to reconcile all men with God and with each other.

A life according to the evangelical counsels of simplicity in service, humility in co-responsibility and celibacy in growing capacity to love is a sign of God's presence in the world and leads to openness for the needs of other men. Those who dedicate themselves totally to the victory of God's love in the world become instruments of reconciliation. It is expected that sisters, brothers and laymen who fully live according to the evangelical counsels should be vigilant for the needs of the discriminated against, the handicapped and drug-addicted, that they be ready to serve in the poor schools of the slums rather than in private schools for the upper middle class. That this is so stems from the fact that a life according to the Sermon on the Mount and in total dedication to it is destined to experience the oneness of the messianic peace and a commitment to peace and genuine human development.

One of the most outstanding examples of such dedication to hope was Brother Albert who worked untiringly to improve the conditions of the poor. He had first been one of the great freedom fighters of Poland; in the course of a battle, he lost a leg. He later on became a famous painter. Everyone found himself at home in his atelier and he did not mind anyone's helping himself freely to whatever he needed. Brother Albert already had a number of "disorderly friends" when he finally decided to take up quarters in the slums of Cracow in a sector of the city so dangerous that even the police dared not penetrate. Before he settled there, Brother Albert had pleaded with the city officials not to use his presence in the slums as a reason for entering and attempting to establish control because he believed in the power of a vulnerable peaceful presence.

Brother Albert did not believe nor did he engage in moralizing corrections. He simply wanted to be present as a brother among brethren and try to improve their housing situation. He organized plays and all kinds of wholesome recreational activities. Through his presence, the gospel of peace became more incarnate in the life of these poor people. Within one year the crime rate in Cracow had fallen by more than 50 per cent. He had succeeded in convincing these people, until now deprived and depraved, that they needed to join forces for the improvement of their living conditions and whole environment.

Once after receiving a substantial sum of money for his work, one of his friends broke his wooden leg, robbed him and disappeared. The thought never even occurred to Brother Albert to denounce him to the police. After a few months the culprit returned; Brother Albert embraced him and said simply: "I knew you would return." Such is the power of hope and peace. It is an incarnate hope that inspires temporal hope even in hopeless situations. Brother Albert's powerful message had opened minds and hearts to a new understanding of Christian hope.

It is not to favor pessimism that I illustrate the same truth by a "skunk" story. Some twenty years ago in Bavaria, a movement called the Bavarian Party wanted to set up a big, ostentatious gambling casino that would attract wealthy people from all over the world. The vocal advocates of this gambling venture were later indicted in connection with bribery charges. In any event, they marshaled every possible argument to prove to parliament the need for such an institution: it would contribute to the income of the state, it would favor man's exercise of freedom, and so on. Some members of the Christian Democratic Party apparently went along with these views. After the case had been skillfully presented, a well-known Socialist stood up and delivered the shortest address ever recorded in the parliament: "And lead us not into temptation."

We cannot yearn for salvation for ourselves if we build a world that leads to temptation or one designed to function with structures and laws at best questionable; all this becomes institutionalized temptation against hope.

Although we can never dispose of the messianic peace as if it were our own achievement, we can nevertheless make an investment of kindness, justice, truthfulness and thus promote peace on earth and render testimony to the power of the messianic peace.

If we ourselves are firmly grounded in hope, we will work patiently and persistently for hope-inspiring conditions of life for others. We cannot comfort people with the hope of eternal life if we remain insensitive or cold to the hungry and the blind, if we are apathetic and unwilling to work for the improvement of the inhumane conditions in many prisons and reformatories. There are wonderful families in Italy and in the United States who, during the past few years, have obtained permission for youths from local prisons to live with their family. I know of one family of seven children that adopted a youngster who had already been tried several times; they extricated him from absolutely inhumane living conditions. He had been arrested for petty thievery; in prison he was repeatedly molested and raped by homosexuals. With the help of this loving family, he has turned into a very promising young man. Had he remained in prison, he would have been thoroughly perverted. I also know of a Protestant minister in the United States who has adopted a young Negro who had been repeatedly sent to prison; I was very impressed by the young man when I met him. He very likely will become a prominent leader in the black community; he is now living in a normal situation.

Shalom is above all the experience of an undeserved gift of God's bounty and therefore invites to gratitude. But since it is a gift of the one Redeemer for the whole world, it comprises an abundance of hope and love. Gratitude will therefore find expression in an unwavering commitment to reconciliation. The task of the whole priestly people of God and particularly of the ministerial

priesthood can be viewed in this perspective of reconciliation.

Christ is the high priest who, in his blood, reconciles
mankind with God and brings further reconciliation on
earth. Those who receive the first fruits of redemption
are enlisted in this service of reconciliation. "What I
mean is, that God was in Christ reconciling the world
to himself, no longer holding man's misdeeds against
them, and that he has entrusted us with the message of
reconciliation. We come therefore as Christ's ambassadors. It is as if God were appealing to you through us:
in Christ's name, we implore you, be reconciled to God!"
(2 Cor. 5:19–20). With these words Paul speaks of his
apostolic service but he also appeals to all the faithful
to follow Christ who, for our sake, made himself one with
the sinfulness of man so that in him we may be one with
the goodness of God himself and build up solidarity in
peace.

Paul appeals to the community of Corinth in these
terms: "Sharing in God's work, we urge this appeal upon
you: you have received the grace of God; do not let it
go for nothing" (2 Cor. 6:1). Paul had to cause tensions
with the Judeo-Christians in order to open the ministry
of reconciliation to all men. But he is most careful not to
create unnecessary tensions and hurts. "In order that our
service may not be brought into discredit, we avoid
giving offence in anything" (2 Cor. 6:3). In restating
the meaning of the ministerial priesthood for this age's
opening up new avenues for the future and unavoidably kindling new tensions, we have to see the organic
unity between reconciliation with God and reconciliation
in the world.

The priest, minister of reconciliation, has to be spirit-
ually and psychologically prepared for the role of peace-
maker without yielding to the temptation of seeking an

easy peace. He must be able to maintain himself in the peace of Christ regardless of the pressures bearing upon him and to communicate this peace to others. In the midst of all the historically new events, he is to apprise others of the totally new event and hope, namely, the messianic peace, reconciliation with God and the hope for final brotherhood. He is to be a minister of peace and unity not only in spite of tensions but in the midst of tensions. The Acts of the Apostles inform us that the early apostolic community was one heart and one mind; yet they do not conceal the growing pains, many tensions and crises through which the dynamics of the messianic peace were still manifest.

Christian hope never accepts a spurious peace; only the false prophets cry out: "Peace! Peace!" where there is crying injustice and lack of sincerity. One needs the courage of the prophets to unmask false peace in order to make way for that peace which comes from God. Christ, the Prince of Peace, is the personification of saving conflict and mediating reconciliation. The ministerial priesthood should serve as exemplar for the whole priestly people of God that they may understand and accept their calling to be ambassadors of true peace. The life of today's priests should particularly proclaim what Paul communicates to the Corinthians in their tensions and dissensions: "Praise be to the God and Father of our Lord Jesus Christ, the all-merciful Father, the God whose consolation never fails us! He comforts us in all our troubles, so that we in turn may be able to comfort others in any trouble of theirs and to share with them the consolation we ourselves receive from God. As Christ's cup of suffering overflows, and we suffer with him, so also through Christ our consolation overflows" (2 Cor. 1:3-5).

Even within the Church, reconciliation is never a *fait accompli* but a task always to be done anew. For the reconciliation of the different trends and currents, it would seem most important to focus on their complementarity. The ongoing reconciliation within the Church should be an example for reconciliation in the world. There can be peace and reconciliation only in a growing respect for pluralism, learning the art of dialogue and accepting, where need be, an open-ended compromise. Are we always aware that we cannot be a source of reconciliation for others unless we personally open ourselves in humble prayer and meditation for the undeserved peace and reconciliation? Only the prayerful man can be a minister of peace.

The messianic peace lies neither in bare horizontalism nor in an abstract verticalism. It is never at home where man seeks only consolation for his own soul nor does it come through those persons who are convinced that by themselves they can build a better world. The messianic peace is more than a social or cultural revolution; it never identifies itself with any specific culture or race. Only a humble Church that serves as bond of unity for all the different trends, schools and cultures can have a good impact on the secular world.

From a perspective of "political theology," we can compare those trends of the Roman Curia that would like to submit theology and the liturgy to the Latin "superculture" with the temptation of the Germanic race that led them to say in past decades: *Am deutschen Wesen soll die Welt genesen;* they imposed the Germanic culture as basis for the measurement of all others. Likewise, there are trends in the United States that claim the right of "messianic calling" for the American nation to be the "leader" and to tell all the other nations, for instance, to adopt their birth-control programs. The Church should be a witness that faith in Christ and the peace he imparts to us liberate man from all such claims and domineering attitudes.

While we stated emphatically that the messianic peace is more than a social gospel, the point must also be made that those who are truly ambassadors of reconciliation with God never fail to work for justice and peace. Yet, the Gospel is never tied up with any economic or political system; it remains always a healthy criticism, an appeal to reform. It never allows one to settle down with the status quo. The messianic peace not only calls for a continuous conversion but it also impels believers to commit themselves to development on all levels. Pope Paul VI has repeatedly expressed the same message in his own way: "Development is a new name for peace."

We celebrate the messianic peace in manifold ways but particularly in the sacrament of penance. We realize more than ever today that the sacrament of reconciliation is not a saving event tied up with a confessional box. The meaningful celebration of the sacrament of penance opens all the horizons of peace, reconciliation and non-violent action. Christians should sometimes be shamed and humbled by the commitment of humanists and men like Mahatma Gandhi for peace and non-violence. Only if Christians absolutely commit themselves to peace can the world realize that Christ alone is peace and that religion is in no way an alienation. The disciples of Christ should be in the vanguard of any peace action; this will be the case if they are true believers.

Believers will not succumb to the illusion that they can construct an earthly paradise. They have the fortitude to face reality, to stand courageously in the midst of tension and to unmask all the idols endangering peace. We should not be unaware of the fact that a rejection of the hope of everlasting life is one of the sources of violence. If this world is our last hope, then it is easy to

understand why men should want to kill each other for
this last hope. But if peace in Christ and the promise of a
final reconciliation sustain our hope, then we will be
ready to work patiently and at the cost of personal sacrifice for the reconciliation of the world. Our peace efforts
cannot be based on some utopian messianism as was the
case with a number of "social gospel" representatives. If
our common commitment to peace is based on the com-
manding view of reconciliation, it will be more realistic
and more humble. Only if we put all our trust in Christ
will we display the necessary endurance and be able to
give credit and trust to each other in an ongoing and
occasionally demanding process of reconciliation.

The revealed truth that "love hopes everything" applies
especially in relation to the daily experiences of human
love: the hope to be loved, a love that hopes the loved one
will fully find his true self. The expressed hope can
awaken an astonishing response in the one who is honored by such trust. If a parent or educator gives credit
to a child or an adolescent, sincere efforts on the latter's
part will reward the parent's trust. If you expect nothing
good from a child, he will deteriorate. The same principle holds true for religious communities. There are cases
of superiors who consistently and constantly need to
prove that they are right in their opposition to a certain
brother or sister. If failure comes, they triumphally cry
out: "I always said so." Little do they realize that the
failure came mainly from the fact that they always
thought and said so. They aborted hope by their lack of
encouragement. The same pedagogical principle could
apply to the faithful with respect to their bishop; if they
give him credit they will often be astounded by how he
manages his difficult task and can be truly a minister of
unity and reconciliation. Those in authority who manifest
a great trust in the work of God's grace and therefore in

the good will of those entrusted to their ministry will experience God's blessing. But those who disseminate suspicion and institutionalize distrust will reap the harvest.

The Apostle of the Gentiles himself once missed this point while his friend Barnabas realized it better. Paul had certainly failed to give Mark credit when the latter had expected it. So Mark left him on the first great missionary journey after the first trying experiences of stoning and imprisonment; today, we would say that Mark took a leave of absence. He later returned with Barnabas, driven by zeal and probably also by a great admiration for Paul. Paul did not readmit him, but later on he did not try to prove he was right. In his Epistle to the Colossians, he comments that of all the people of the circumcision, nobody works so well for the Gospel as Mark (Col. 4:11). To Timothy, he writes to bring back Mark with him because he needs his help (2 Tim. 4:11). That Mark developed into a great missionary is due to the encouragement of Barnabas who gave him credit when Paul did not; later Paul did give credit to Mark and he deserved it. This is the kind of human experience that is rooted in faith, in God's grace; it is conducive to a better and more vital appreciation of what trust in God means. In my opinion, such a human experience holds a "sacramental grace" because it is by God's creative and redemptive presence that we can perceive the connection between human trust and the hope that comes from God and leads to him. A hope of eternal life that is incarnate is tremendously relevant; it includes temporal hope, mutual trust and encouragement inspired by ever greater hope. The peace of Christ can and will be the greatest force on earth if his disciples only make visible the fact that it bears fruit for the life of the world on all levels and on every occasion.

13

THE ESCHATOLOGICAL VIRTUES

Central to every form of Christian witness are faith, love and the eschatological virtues. It is through Greek influence that the four cardinal virtues gained prominence in our moral teaching and set the direction of ascetical life. The fundamental thrust of the Bible does not come from prudence, self-control, fortitude and justice; the Bible is oriented toward hope. The eucharist reminds us anew of the fundamental outlook of the Christian: hope in thanksgiving and hope in vigilance for present opportunities, for the coming of the Lord here and now and for his final coming.

Hope serves as the hub of the wheel of Christian virtues. Faith and love need to be permeated with hope because of the pilgrim situation in which the disciples of Christ find themselves. The Christian knows that he cannot attain final fulfillment on earth, but he knows equally well how decisive this earthly life is with respect to final fulfillment. Hope is the indispensable dynamic force of faith and love.[1] Christian hope is based on loving *gratitude* for God's magnificent gifts and deeds. Without

[1] See Chapter 6, "The Dynamism of Hope: Faith Active in Love."

constant thanksgiving and praise, there is no freedom
from anguish, bitterness and anger, no way of giving
salvific and healing meaning to the many unavoidable
frustrations.

It has been a very heartening experience for me to
meet so many sisters and priests from different "houses of
prayer." Among these religious and clerics there is a pre-
vailing spirit of praise and gratitude; there is no room for
bitterness and angry polarizations in these groups. It is
not that these priests and sisters have become uncritical
but their discernment is based on gratitude, appreciation
and trust.

Gratitude is a function of the Christian outlook of
hope; one imbued with hope renders thanks always and
everywhere. The model is Christ himself who, en route to
Calvary, gives thanks to his Father for having sent him in
poverty to be the obedient Servant in the great design of
the salvation of mankind. The distinctive characteristic
of the Christian shaped by the eucharist is his ability to
render thanks for all things in all situations; he can sing
the Canticle of the Sun, he can praise God even for
Brother Death and for his human frailty.

In a parish where I had been preaching, I was surprised to find a great spirit of faith and such responsive-
ness on the part of the people to the point that I queried
the pastor: "Can you tell me what you have done to bring
about such openness? How do you account for it? I
have noticed a unique spirit of faith, of trust and zeal."
He replied at once: "Neither I nor my curate is responsible, though he is a good man. You must go and see a
certain spinster who has renewed the parish." I accepted
the suggestion and paid her a visit; she had been bedrid-
den for over twenty years. Even with great effort, she
could not move her arms and hands sufficiently to feed
herself. She was totally dependent on others for all per-

sonal care. However she was radiantly at peace and her
peace of mind was a source of inspiration, trust and faith
for the whole parish. I asked her to explain to me the
source of her joy. "When this illness struck me, I made a
pilgrimage to Lourdes expecting a miraculous cure but
when I saw all the suffering, I asked God to let me offer
this affliction for the salvation of the world. Since then,
I have come to understand better what a joy it is to be
able to offer something of myself with Christ for the
salvation of mankind." The tiny room of that virgin lady
was the center of the whole parish; it radiated a spirit of
faith and gratitude even amid great suffering. She could
live joyfully because she was so fully united with Christ.

The true Christian gratefully accepts whatever happens to him in any given situation. During November of
last year, death claimed one of my dearest friends, a
confrère ninety-three years old; he had earlier asked me
to give him extreme unction when he felt his last hour
had come. I complied and spent the night with him.
About three hours after receiving the sacrament, he re-
covered his voice and asked: "Tell me, what is the name
of the author who wrote that magnificent book, Ita,
Pater?" I told him: Father Graeff. "Now is the moment
for my last 'Yes, Father.'" I then asked him how he felt.
"I am very happy; I am so happy . . ." and these were
his last words. This elderly man had truly accepted the
spirit of Vatican II and all the ensuing changes as something he had always hoped for all his life.

The Christian spirit of gratitude is one that can accept
change; it is a gratitude rooted in the Paschal Mystery
where selfishness is put to death, where the horizon is
open, where man has gained his freedom to serve the
whole people of God in Christ. The eucharist connotes
the full dimension of his gratitude in hope. When the
Christian looks back he does not do so with a sour face

like the wife of Lot; he looks back in thankfulness marveling at the wondrous deeds of God. His thanksgiving for the daily events is staked on the manifestation of God's love, in the passion, death and resurrection of the Lord. Thus, with a gratitude based on God's fidelity, on everything he has done, the Christian can look back, knowing that God, who has so wonderfully begun his work in creation, is pursuing it in an ineffable way in Jesus Christ and will fulfill it in him on the day of the Parousia. So it is a celebration of hope in thanksgiving and a celebration of gratitude in hope.

By looking back on the great deeds of God and waiting for the final fulfillment, the Christian is not alienating himself from the reality of life. He is always ready to fathom the full import of the present moment because he knows that here and now he is meeting Christ in his brothers and sisters and in all of God's children. The Christian loves the whole world with Christ's love; he discovers the mark of salvation in human history. So his thanksgiving and hope will not allow him to be alienated or estranged from life. Rather, they commit him in a redeeming way to the world which yearns for a share in the freedom gained by gratitude and liberating hope.

Gratitude and hope yield *vigilance for the kairos;* it is an essential and basic principle of Christian ethics to be alert for the present opportunities. "The hymn says: 'Sleeper awake; rise from the dead and Christ will shine upon you.' Use to the fullest the present opportunity" (Eph. 5:14–16). If we are awake, if we gratefully grasp the full import of God's work and words and if we view all events with hope and as leading toward final fulfillment, then it is impossible to live the present moment superficially and distractedly; it must be lived with the light of Christ shining upon us. We can then perceive the wealth and depth of the here-and-now, the real oppor-

tunities to serve our brethren and to praise God in our
daily work and encounters.

The Christian does not live in an "if-and-but" world
but with a daily "Yes, Father, here I am" to the Lord's
calling. He accepts the limited possibilities and patiently
bears the heat of the day; he can equally well adjust to
the chilly weather and the depressing moments of life,
exhibiting a trust that transcends the painful moment.
As human beings and sons of Adam, we always have a
certain propensity to escape and become alienated from
reality, but when we are led by the spirit of Christ we are
set free for the real task. Through the gifts of the Holy
Spirit, we can recognize all the gifts God has given us as
an appeal, a gracious invitation to serve our brethren.
The liturgy helps us to see things in a broader light and
helps to place in perspective daily realities; it teaches us
the great art of being realistic and truly sets us on the
path with the Lord. We are not encapsulated forever in
the present moment; this would represent an Establishment attitude, the end of all hope. We look forward, living in the present tense while keeping an eye on the future.

Another eschatological virtue fundamentally rooted in
the Bible is *readiness to change,* the willingness to learn
and unlearn in fidelity to the Lord of history. It refers to
our common prerogative which bears the stamp of God's
guarantee: the privilege to err or to make mistakes. This
should motivate us to cultivate the most important attitude in this respect, namely, the courage to make mistakes. I have a very gifted friend who can read and understand a number of foreign languages but he has never
learned to speak a second language because of his fear
of mistakes. We learn very little if we do not risk making mistakes. Parents who do not allow their children or
teenagers ever to make mistakes are merely educating

them for infantilism. All of us have the right and privilege
to err, but this does not mean that we must indulge in
calculated mistakes. In our effort to do what is right, we
must run the risk of being mistaken occasionally; it is all
part of the learning process. It is equally the privilege of
the Roman Catholic Church to err because she is a pilgrim Church. We should not be so niggardly as to deprive
bishops and the dear Holy Father himself of their good
right to err occasionally.

In the fourteenth century, Pope John XXII taught that
the separated souls would not see God before the Parousia. It was a great mistake for which he was blamed and
immediately censured by theologians; he did not com-
plicate the issue but apologized. In his testament he
stated that if he had erred, he felt sure God would forgive him because he had made the mistake through simple ignorance and not out of arrogance. This is true Christian humility, an attitude that could ultimately make the
institution of the papacy acceptable for our separated
brethren. If all Christians and all Churches adopted a
humble attitude, it would greatly help eliminate bitterness. We have a serious problem posed today by the
millions of self-styled "infallible popes," people who criticize violently and are very intolerant because they are
not aware of their own limitations. If we all enjoy the
privilege of making mistakes, we also have the corresponding duty to acknowledge our mistakes and correct
them.

Readiness to change arises from and leads to fidelity if
it is in harmony with the perspective indicated by the
Paschal Mystery, which we commemorate and celebrate
in the eucharist. Change should not be merely for the
sake of change nor for making detours, but change should
be based on our longing to find the best entrance to the
Lord's highways. Consequently, our changes should be

the result of meditation, prayer and painstaking effort to know the real situation, the alternatives offered to us in the here-and-now in order to find the most appropriate step leading toward final fulfillment. It means a readiness to change in fidelity to the Lord of history; as creative fidelity, it necessarily entails the courage of risk in humility. No doubt exists that those who vigorously promote ecumenism are taking risks in view of the hope for unifying all Christians. Mistakes are made and will be made in this effort, but infinitely greater is the risk of settling for lifelessness and separateness forever. If the Church dare not take risks, she will be at worst a graveyard, and at best a run-down refuge for old people. We can take the risks of life only with prayer, humility and that courage which arises from trust in God. Life and risks are possible only if we finally entrust ourselves to the Lord of history, trusting fully that he is guiding us and healing us.

Epikeia represents the courage to take risks in the realm of traditional teaching. Those who exhibit this virtue know well that it is wrong to cling to the letter of the law for security's sake when it is against the great law of love in responsibility. St. Thomas Aquinas finds that the adult Christian striving toward maturity is duty-bound to prefer a possible error by seeking the spirit of the law to the committing of a very probable error against the law of love by clinging to the letter of the law. If we rigidly abide by the letter of the law without attempting to search for its deeper spirit, we have not yet reached even the minimal level of morality. I find it a sign of hope that so many Christians today are yearning for a more profound understanding of the Lord's great commandment of love and its articulation in daily life; they thereby indicate willingness to assume risks with new ventures. However, we must not take risks about important matters without prayer and without examining our conscience and motives, asking ourselves whether or not we have done our best (not the impossible) to know the full situation. We must learn to discern in the light of the full scale and urgency of human values.

Another eschatological virtue, therefore, is *discernment* with respect to complex present-day historical situations. Discernment presupposes a constant readiness to learn what constitute the proper criteria for carrying on a dialogue with others while being respectfully docile to the magisterium. Discernment must always be exercised in solidarity with a view to building up the Mystical Body; it calls for a distinction between what is in accord with the law of growth and the total vocation of man and how best under the present circumstances to serve God and to give witness to him, the Lord of history, while remaining sensitive to the needs and real possibilities of people.

A distinctly eschatological virtue which seems to have been rediscovered in our own day is that of *non-violence*, which may be defined as the patient and firm action on behalf of a more just and humane world without ever resorting to inhumane means. This is one of the most important virtues or attitudes contributing to Church renewal and helping promote a genuinely Christian "revolution" in the world that looks forward to more humane conditions.

Karl Marx was convinced that only by feeding class hatred and increasing tension, by preparing for a final explosion of violence, would mankind attain perfect harmony, peace, brotherhood and unselfishness for which the proletariat longed. His theories were a strange mixture of so-called science and apocalyptic prophecy. The Christian hopes for a world of justice and peace, that is, a humane world and one of brotherhood beyond this

world, but this very hope determines the goal and means
of his commitment. He is committed to working for a
non-violent revolution in the spirit of the Gospel. When
the disciples of Christ try to be good, kind and merciful
to each other, like God who revealed his goodness and
mercy in Jesus Christ, we witness a very radical kind of
transformation indeed. A Gospel-based revolution seeks
that kind of action, those structures and publicly shared
convictions that promote non-violence on all sides.

We are committed to the world because of our hope for
peace in Christ. We believe that the messianic peace has
already appeared to us in Christ and that Christ leads us
by his own non-violent actions, the highest form of activity, toward a total commitment to peace on earth.

There are great hopes for but also serious threats to
progress in non-violent attitudes and action in our day.
Gandhi was certainly a man who, in a quite extraordinary
way, embodied non-violence, co-operation for peace and
justice and absolute respect for the human dignity of all
men; his inspirations flowed from his firm hope. He laid
down the certain conditions for non-violent action. A deep
union with God was the first; therefore, at the very outset
of his career, he founded an *ashram*, a house of prayer.
A second essential demanded a constructive plan; non-
violence was never to be understood as a mere tactic—it
had to be a spirituality, an abiding attitude of respect and
love. Non-violent protest and action do honor to those
against whom they are directed; the protest informs them
that they have not been written off as unimportant.
Gandhi believed that we must never give up hope that
those who today oppress and oppose us will some day be
our friends. He achieved this goal with eventual friendship between the Indian and the British peoples. This is
certainly one of the greatest achievements of this century.

Martin Luther King is another example of non-violence

who still has many followers; our hopes and the times call for still more followers. In Brazil Archbishop Helder Camara is one of the great forces for justice and united non-violent action. He is right in warning that violence will of necessity increase unless a common effort is made on all sides vigorously to promote justice by all non-violent means. Inaction on one side and the oppressive use of power on the other will result in violent explosions without truly freeing man. Bishop Camara is as convinced as was Gandhi of the necessity of that kind of prayer life which is the source of hope nourishing the spirit of non-violence in action. A house of prayer, intended to be a school of prayer and non-violence, is now being set up in Recife.

Non-violence belongs to one of the seven solemn words of the Lord in Matthew 5: "But I tell you . . ." (For the Christian, these take the place of the "ten words"—the Decalogue.) It can be the greatest force, a great strength, but only if it is rooted in unlimited hope. When hope is fading away, non-violent action becomes a mere technique and can explode into new forms of violence or into the hypocritical use of seemingly non-violent tactics in a violent spirit.

Non-violence is more than a technique that can be learned. However, there are aspects that can be mastered; there must be a place for the charisms of intuition, imagination and design, but the source of strength remains hope. The basis lies in that deep union with God, trusting that those who walk with God in peace can be peacemakers. However, it also entails a willingness to pay the cost of discipleship; this spells the real difference between a Christian understanding of non-violence and non-violence as a bare political technique or tactic.

14
ACTING ON THE WORD

Toward the end of the Gospel of St. John, there is a startling story about a little misunderstanding, which helps us appreciate more the deeper meaning of Christian life. Once Peter had been reconciled beside the Lake of Tiberias, reassured in his friendship with the Lord and confirmed in his ministry of unity, he "looked around and saw the disciple whom Jesus loved following—the one who at supper had leaned back close to him to ask the question, 'Lord, who is it that will betray you?' When he caught sight of him, Peter asked, 'Lord, what will happen to him?'" (Jn. 21:20–21). Peter seems to feel that John was more deserving than he was of the ministry of unity because he had stood the test of loyalty far better. Peter has obviously lost his excessive trust in himself; it is no longer the Peter of "Everyone else may fall away but I will not" (Mk. 14:29). Peter had experienced the power of the Lord's mercy, of the Lord's Passion and now asks: "What will become of him?" Jesus answers: "If it should be my will that he wait until I come, what is it to you? Follow me" (Jn. 21:22).

"That saying of Jesus became current in the brotherhood, and was taken to mean that that disciple would not die. But in fact, Jesus did not say that he would not die; he only said, 'If it should be my will that he wait until I come, what is it to you?' It is this same disciple who attests what has been written here" (Jn. 21:23–24). John, with the penetrating eye of the eagle, recognizes the Lord when he comes under any disguise; he is the witness to the Gospel and for the Gospel of hope. The Lord did not say that John would not die before the Parousia: he said something more. He revealed the character and charism of John to be one of constantly waiting for the coming of the Lord in all events, with Christ-like vigilance and love for his neighbors and the needs of the community.

The whole Church could be transformed if this episode were properly understood. It is said to Peter: "What is it to you?" Peter cannot understand his ministry as Supreme Shepherd without John, that is, without that other ministry or charism of John that should characterize the whole Church even in her institutional aspects: waiting for the coming of the Lord. An enlightening parallelism could be drawn comparing this episode in the Gospel of St. John with chapters 3, 5 and 6 of the conciliar document on the Church, *Lumen gentium,* which deal with the ministry of the pope and the bishops and the charism of those totally dedicated to the kingdom of God through the charism of the evangelical counsels.

The eschatological virtues mentioned in the preceding chapter are particularly indispensable for persons called to live according to the evangelical counsels. Celibacy for the heavenly kingdom and the evangelical witness to poverty can be lived only by those who behold the great vision of gratitude, hope and docility to the Holy Spirit. The counsels entail vigilance with respect to the here-and-now, a readiness to change direction in response to the fidelity of the living God of history, and the courage to take risks. Everything flows from the evangelical spirit of *poverty*, the gift of the Holy Spirit who renews hearts and the face of the earth. Poverty must be understood in the light of that great witness to heaven, Christ, who was in the divinity the Word of God but who, in the greatest miracle of freedom, makes himself a servant. He obediently fulfills the great design of the Father to manifest the full extent and depth of his love (Phil. 2:6–8). Rich as he was, he made himself poor in order to enrich all of us by his poverty. Christ made himself the Servant Messiah so as to express his fullness and the plenitude of his love, emptying himself of everything but love and loving us even to death on the cross. The spirit of poverty receives its strongest testimony in the very last word of Jesus: "Father, into your hands I commit my spirit."

Those who dedicate themselves to a life according to the evangelical counsels commit themselves above all to a continuous conversion, a constant openness to the Spirit and a readiness to empty themselves of whatever impinges on their liberty or on their freedom to serve and to love unselfishly. The highest values cannot be possessed by power; they are the free gifts of God bestowed upon those who open themselves humbly and gratefully to them.

Everyday experience proves that if we want to love a person truly, we must above all respect that person's freedom. If we try to force a person to love us or want to possess that person, we can never elicit the free response that is love; love is a response in freedom. So poverty must permeate our whole lives, whether it be in marriage or in religious life. Poverty means freedom to serve, the freedom to sense the needs of others, a freedom which respects and guarantees the freedom of other persons, assuring them that they will never be instrumentalized or devoured.

Evangelical poverty is not a discrete entity apart from hope and love; it is the initial manifestation of joy, the wealth of a person who knows that he is truly loved by the greatest lover, Christ. It is the realization that all things, especially our capacities, are marvelous gifts, a tremendous wealth, because they are more than mere possessions. They are signs of God's own love and signs of his goodness, thus promises and signs of hope. Therefore, any person who, with all that he is and all that he has, places himself at the service of his brethren, the service of the common good, is a "sacrament," a remarkable sign and witness of eschatological hope. Such a person shows gratitude for things already begun, proclaims the wealth of love already manifest and hopes for the plenitude of love yet unseen but guaranteed by God. This helps him to make the best possible use of present opportunities and possibilities for action, even very modest and insignificant occasions.

Christ himself is the witness to heaven, the witness to hope because of his *obedience*. His is not a slavish obedience, however, but an expression of the highest degree of freedom; he freely binds himself to his brethren agreeing to be their servant and Redeemer. It is one of the noblest manifestations of man's freedom to be able to bind himself to fidelity by conjugal vows, religious vows or any other great, irrevocable commitment. Such an act is a tremendous exercise of freedom but one that needs revitalization every day. Such a commitment cannot be assured once and for all by a "yes" at the altar on the wedding day; the spouses have to learn and constantly relearn the meaning of genuine love. When illusions have collapsed and the very core of the other person becomes exposed, then is the time to realize that one's earlier "yes" freely uttered really commits him to further growth in freedom now, growth in depth and in courage. The situa-

tion is very similar in the case of religious vows; like
Moses setting out and looking forward, the religious will
find new horizons opening up, but the true religious will
accept the daily insecurities because of his firm trust in
God which gives him a sense of security that has nothing
in common with the security complex of those who are
always anxiously seeking themselves.

Obedience opens our eyes to the needs of the community. One who makes a commitment of obedience becomes the freest servant imaginable since he intends only
to serve, to guarantee the dignity of each person in the
community and to promote the unity and solidarity of all.
Mature obedience inspires hope in the person who is fully
committed to the common good. Disobedience can be a
fault in leaders as well as in non-leaders; the difference
is only one of degree although it might express itself in a
variety of ways. For instance, those leaders or religious
superiors who will not allow persons gifted with charisms
such as good ideas, imagination, a sense of humor or the
ability to criticize constructively to place their talents,
their wealth, at the service of the common good are
truly disobedient. Leaders must be eminently obedient
to the common good and the welfare of the group; they
must stand ready always to examine their motives in the
form of service expected of them. In certain cases it may
be that the highest form of obedience in service to the
common good is to retire; this could well represent the
superior's or bishop's last great contribution to the community. Today, religious are in general a sign of hope;
most congregations have by now eliminated their "eternal fathers" and "eternal mothers." Such courage should
inspire the Church to free herself from "eternal bishops."

It is a great sign of vigilance and obedience to the
common good when a bishop resigns at the proper moment. The question asked of young men being ordained

to the priesthood: "Do you promise obedience?" should be understood as: "Do you promise obedience to the common good?" This includes obedience to the legitimate bearer of authority who, in turn, must be able to obey and to submit himself in all things to the dictates of the common good.

Many religious orders and congregations have paved the way. They elect their superior general or general minister for six years, after which he becomes Father Cooke or Father Schmidt like any other; this is freedom in service. After serving the community for six years as a major superior, he is freed to serve it in the most humble and loving way, and the community, in turn, is free to look for the best new servant of unity and servant of the common good. Closely related to this power of freedom is the concept of *collegiality* which liberates those in the service of unity from all forms of isolation, allowing them to share each other's experiences, to exchange reflections and insights systematically and thus to know and be in a better position to serve the community. Such a sharing of experiences is authentic obedience because it fosters a genuine freedom to serve the common good.

One of my first sessions in the confessional brought me a precious experience of how to understand obedience. A male penitent came to me and said: "I was disobedient to my wife." I told him candidly that I was quite inexperienced as a confessor, that I was learning and needed his help. "We were always told that the wife is to obey the husband. Why do you confess that you disobeyed your wife?"—"Oh, Father, it was quite clear: she was right!" I must add that my gentleman was a little uneasy when I asked him: "Would you accept as penance telling your wife that she was right?" History abounds with stories illustrating the point that it is difficult for those bound by certain traditions and structures to recognize that others are right. A pope, a bishop or a religious superior is truly free and serves freely the people under him if he does not think only of his own superiority but recognizes genuine authority in those who can point convincingly to the best way of serving the common good. We have then a display of evangelical obedience in the exercise of authority.

Whenever I refer to the witness of *chastity*, I intend to include premarital and conjugal chastity, the chastity of the widow and of divorced persons, and the consecrated chastity of those who dedicate themselves to the Gospel or to the service of the needy. Chastity confers great freedom. If we thirst and hunger for God's rightful rule to prevail, if we appreciate union with God as the highest good, if we respect the person of others and revere them as children of God, then chastity becomes for us a source of hope and harvest of hope. Chastity strengthens hope just as hope strengthens chastity. I am not referring to any kind of reward for oneself for having renounced the joys of the world; I do not consider sour old maids or cantankerous bachelors as "virgins." I consider eminently chaste those who are able to love without consuming or possessing the other person, who can love in freedom and also receive love in absolute freedom. Celibacy for the sake of the Kingdom means a completely radical decision never to possess another person.

In Christian marriage the mystery emerges also when the marriage has truly become a sign of union and hope. The great Protestant theologian Karl Barth considers it a serious duty of the Christian minister to alert young people to the two great possibilities of choice before them: they can either serve God in celibacy for his kingdom or serve him in marriage. He is convinced that if we no longer have the witness of those who have embraced celibacy for the heavenly kingdom in great freedom, then many people will feel "condemned to marriage." Single girls and bachelors would then become the "left-overs" of marriage choices. Barth's statement strongly supports the witness of religious men and women for freedom. It is because of the joy of the Gospel and that deep realization that God has given the celibate so many signs of love that he does not feel bound to one way of life, namely, that of serving God in marriage albeit a very great and meritorious way. Marriage is also a calling to holiness, but unless there is freedom inspired by trust in God and hope in everlasting life, neither marriage nor celibacy can be considered a vocation because the latter presupposes the free choice of a state of life. Both must witness to that hope which stems from gratitude for all that God has given us. In marriage we rightly expect to encounter chastity that preserves the freedom of the other person and never consumes or uses the other person as an object.

In some circles, there is much senseless talk about self-fulfillment; there are claims made that one cannot fulfill himself unless he has an exclusive friend or companion of the opposite sex. This is tantamount to devouring the other person and leads unavoidably to mutual frustration. Genuine friendship is characterized by reverence and is respectful of the other person's life and calling.

The life of one of the greatest German theologians, Johann Adam Möhler, was a marvelous witness to this kind of freedom. His famous book on the Church already breathed the spirit of Vatican II more than a century ago. Möhler was a seminarian and during his last long vacation before becoming a subdeacon, he met a wonderful young lady with whom he fell in love. They came to a mutual confession of love for each other. In all sincerity, the young girl asked him if he had been sure of his calling to the priesthood before meeting her. The young man replied as sincerely: "Yes, I was sure." She then admitted: "I will never possess you against your true vocation." This noble gesture helped him see his celibate priestly vocation in a new light, as freedom to renounce a selfish desire, trusting that what God wanted was greater than a beautiful human dream.

Those who truly live the evangelical counsels, therefore, constitute a sign of hope for the world; their way of life manifests the great freedom to love in the way of Christ. Christ did not come to build a home for his own family but to dedicate himself to the whole family of God. However, religious life must be seen in an absolutely unifying perspective with the witness of Christian spouses who are searching for the will of God in all things. They are companions on pilgrimage toward eternal life; they communicate to their children through unselfish love the gladdening news of God who is in their midst as their redeeming partner and companion on the path preparing for eternal life.

The present period of turmoil, transition and renewal signals the need of the Church for the great witness to fidelity and hope provided by religious men and women who unceasingly strive to be credible signs of the liberating power, joy and love which enable each to answer his or her own calling and to serve with the fullness of one's personality. If we believe in the resurrection of the Lord, namely, that death in Christ is the highest expression of freedom, preparing us for the great revelation of the resurrection, then it makes sense to live according to the evangelical counsels and to be a witnessing sign for the pilgrim Church, singing hymns and songs, and rendering thanks to God.

In this light, I feel that a life fully in accord with the evangelical counsels can be a hopeful "yes" to God's word, to God's work and to his world, because it is directed toward the final fulfillment which is the fullest freedom and the all-embracing power of unselfish love. A life based on the evangelical counsels can help to restore that freedom which God originally planned and which Christ came to restore. It can manifest the beginning of the final fulfillment. It can be a forceful "yes" to life and to that freedom guaranteed by Christ.

How blessed are those who come to that freedom in which they wholeheartedly adore not only by words but by their whole being the absolute freedom of God to guide and transfigure us. Man reaches his greatest hope on earth when he removes all obstacles to God's gracious action.

15

HOPE FOR THE "HOPELESS"

When I hear pastors or superiors speaking about "hopeless cases," I cannot help but reflect: Where is their faith in God? Where is their hope? According to the optimistic outlook of the Gospel, there is truly no hopeless case, no hopeless situation; God calls everybody to forgiveness and repentance.

I am thinking especially of the situation of homosexuals, drug addicts, drunkards or people suffering from any kind of neurotic or other psychopathological weakness. Psychology has helped us come to a better understanding of their difficulties; we know that the attitude "you are a hopeless case" only helps to promote their feelings of inadequacy and misery. If we give them credit, if we respect them as persons and appreciate any positive step in the direction of change, they can respond with greater alacrity. Their efforts are highly valued by God, more so perhaps than our seemingly bigger steps because God always looks to good will.

With homosexuals, we must carefully distinguish voluntary perversion from a weakness which can be a source of great suffering. Some years ago I wrote a series of articles in an Italian periodical about the problems of *masturbation* and *homosexuality*. I insisted on how important it was to distinguish between sin and suffering. The afflicted person very often needs to be helped to accept the great suffering of sex deviancy; the painful experience is often intensified by an inability to distinguish between the extent of guilt and the degree of illness; such people must therefore be comforted for any display of good will. When there is good will, an initial effort and acceptance of suffering, there is a basis for hope, a sign of God's saving presence. I was cheered by the responses to my series, including visits and letters. One correspondent wrote: "I was at the point of hanging myself as useless for this world. I am a poor homosexual; I now realize that even this dirty sickness can be a part of redemption and I am relieved. I know now that I am not a hopeless case." If we can get the afflicted person to look at the problem in this light, there is no reason to doubt that therapy would be successful.

Many homosexuals can be helped and possibly cured if instead of passing judgment on them we differentiate between sin and suffering, between what can be eliminated and what must be accepted. More preventive and rehabilitative measures are needed; psychological help must be available to all who cannot obtain help from qualified educators, pastors and ministers. Appropriate motivation and more positive attitudes toward helping the psychologically impaired person will help make Christian morality more credible to modern man than the passing of harsh judgments and issuing of imperatives based on an inadequate knowledge of man and the world. The shocking problems of homosexuality, drug addiction and other psychopathological tendencies call for a more constructive approach based on a painstaking scientific study of the causes.

A few years ago, I conducted a workshop for Italian social workers. The group was organized by a sister of Father Lombardi and Mrs. Merlin, a member of the Socialist party; these social workers were totally dedicated to the rehabilitation of women abused in *prostitution*. During the entire workshop I did not once hear the word "prostitutes" mentioned; they were referred to as "friends" out of respect for the dignity of the person. They described their approach to these women in serious need of help. When their clients succeeded in limiting their sexual contacts to one man, the case worker expressed grateful delight over the first success. However, when expressing appreciation for this progress and thanking them for their effort, they made the client realize that it was a reassuring indication that she was now ready for the next step forward. They encouraged the women to further progress by telling them what they could be in time; they were given an understanding of their worth as persons and of their potential for a good marriage. These seventy social workers are continuing to do marvelous work because of their respect inspired totally by their faith in a God of mercy and Redeemer of all. No one is excluded in the Savior's plan; he came to save all, and the redeeming action of Christ can be communicated better if we know the totality of a person's difficulties, her psychological make-up, the limited possibilities of her environment and the heritage and burden from the past. However, within this realm, miracles can happen especially when there is evidence of hope and faith in those attempting to assist their weaker brethren.

When I was still teaching near Munich, I would from time to time hear the confession of a converted Magdalen. She had been persuaded to lead a better life by a reformed Magdalen who had become a great apostle. Once the dignity of these women has been rescued and they are confirmed in Christ's friendship, they approach other Magdalens, bringing them the hope that is rooted in faith and gratitude. Even when they fall again and return for help, there must be praise for God who never abandons persons in need but gives them strength to start anew. Each effort and each contact is a sign that God wants to renew that person.

A very serious problem is posed by our present *judicial and penal systems*. In spite of considerable progress, the courts still observe double standards; we have laws for the poor and others for the rich or influential. Minor transgressions of the law by the poor fill the court records while the rich man pays for an "off-the-record" settlement. Youths jailed for petty thievery or other minor offenses usually become perverted and frustrated in jail. Our society should be less pharisaical. What is needed is a sounder pedagogical and rehabilitative approach that would enlist the co-responsibility of all the members of society and its institutions. It behooves concerned citizens to suggest and take steps to introduce legislation that will support the rehabilitative efforts of the social agencies. A trained worker coming from a rehabilitation center is often refused employment because of a prison record and/or a history of drug addiction. In such cases, we have the legislative branch of the local or state government working at cross-purposes with the judicial and penal branch for which they appropriate money. The readiness with which we condemn transgressors of our social and juridical norms is too often associated with a comfortable "easy" conscience on the part of the citizens. A more constructive approach would regard the social problems or evils of drug addiction, prostitution and homosexuality as an appeal to renew our sense of co-responsibility and to work for the reform of social structures.

The problem of *remarried persons who had been di-*

vorced is under serious study today; there are a number of books and many articles on this topic. I refer to a few of my own articles one of which was published in *The Jurist:* "Internum Forum Solutions for Insoluble Marriage Cases."[1] Such cases are "insoluble" but not hopeless; they may be without solution for canonists in view of the present system of canon law but a law cannot be the last word for men of good will; such people must be offered a solution of hope, good news for a sincere conscience. If a couple is living together in peace and a separation would harm either party or be a cause of hardship for others, we cannot advise them to leave one another. In most instances, they cannot convince themselves that they should try to live together in total continence (as brother and sister). The harmony of their life together and the peace of an upright conscience demand a resolution in understanding.

Two years ago a Sicilian gentleman came to me together with his brother to discuss his marital problems. I indicated the possibility of moving to another room so as to be able to discuss the matter privately with him. But he objected saying that his brother knew of his plight; he wanted him to hear the discussion because he had been the only person to help him. In brief, the details of the situation were as follows. When he returned from the war he found that his young wife had had two children by other men. He offered to be reconciled and adopt the two children but she refused on both counts. His brother repeatedly acted as go-between reiterating that all would be forgiven but she declined his offer and never returned. Since his brother had many children he

[1] Bernard Häring, "Internum Forum Solutions for Insoluble Marriage Cases," *The Jurist* (January 1970), 21–30. See also my other article, "Pastoral Work Among the Divorced and Invalidly Married," *Concilium* 55 (May 1970), 123–30.

could not be accommodated in that home, so he lived alone, forcibly an isolated being. As time went on, he felt it would be better for him to remarry but this could not be in the Church. He now has eight children. His brother assured me that he had never missed mass; he and his wife never forgot their evening prayer; they prayed the rosary together in spite of their being excluded from the sacraments. I gave him absolution, after which I contacted the bishop of that diocese and told him I had given absolution to the gentleman.

It is a scandal to exclude such good men from the sacramental life of the Church. However, since most people are not yet prepared to understand exceptional cases, I advised the Sicilian to receive communion where he was not known. As far as my experience goes, there is a growing consensus that we should educate people to mature discernment. Then nobody would cry "scandal" when these people receive communion because nobody can doubt their good will. Whether or not these marriage problems can be properly regulated according to canon law is another matter. In many cases the first marriage was probably never a valid one. The present continuing revision of canon law should seek to facilitate matters for many people in the future. It is very obvious that my Sicilian gentleman could not be expected to leave the mother of his children. Together they have worked out their communion as a sign of fidelity, trust and mutual care, and they are the messengers of faith and hope for their children.

Another problematic marriage situation came to my attention two years ago in the United States while I was on an East Coast engagement addressing a large group of Confraternity of Christian Doctrine teachers. A young man about twenty years old came to me and asked if I would have time to see his father; he did not feel he could carry on much longer. I immediately asked for details about his situation. He replied: "We are eight boys; when my mother died, I was twelve and the oldest. My father tried hard to find a mother for us but no Catholic woman wanted to inherit such a herd of boys. Every housekeeper left because things kept going from bad to worse. Finally, an Anglican lady who had been divorced years earlier but who lived a good life had compassion, married him and accepted us all; my brothers have received her well. She is the most marvelous person we could have hoped for. The Sunday following his marriage, my father was an usher in church; the pastor devoted his whole sermon to him, condemning him to the deepest hell. At home, we now have order and there is love in our family; only, my father is becoming more and more depressed." I told the young man to have his father come see me. When he called, I could only say: "What more could I ask of you now?" As in the previous case, he had never missed mass; he saw to the proper education of his children. His oldest son would not have been in CCD work if the father had not cared for them. This family also prayed together. I gave him absolution and told him not to show up in his parish as it was not a sign of hope for him. He could receive communion somewhere else where there would be no loveless talk and no scandal.

The problem with which the Church is grappling today is whether a marriage which is *hopelessly* destroyed imposes lifelong celibacy on the abandoned spouse. Where there is still a possibility of restoring it, we must imitate God's covenant with his people and regard it as irrevocable. He grants forgiveness whenever his people return to him, and he tirelessly calls men to repentance and promises forgiveness. Similarly, as long as a marriage can be saved, it must be saved.

But if the marriage is thoroughly dissolved with no hope of reviving it, then the question is not so much whether we can tear asunder what God has put together as "was it ever put together by God in the first place?" In many instances we have good reason to suspect that the marriage was not put together by God because of the gap between the spouses which could never possibly be bridged. Was this colored girl in New York destined by God for this seventeen-year-old boy who got her pregnant when she was only sixteen? The mother forced the girl to marry him in church. The following night, he pulled out a knife and assaulted her; she still wears the scars from those deep wounds. After a few months she ran away, frightened, because of his repeated threats to her life. The ecclesiastical marriage court says: Nothing can be done since the marriage was performed in church. There is at least a 99 per cent probability that such a marriage was never ordained by God and only a very remote probability that it was; canonists should take this into consideration. Now this poor girl had a history of drug addiction. A group of nuns took the girl into their community in an effort to rehabilitate her, but she will surely return to drugs if she cannot remarry. We have to look at the whole situation. Morality is for people; if our laws and the application of moral principles do not express a concern for people, they are not promoting the common good.

Tradition shows that the Oriental Churches, which constituted the great part of Christendom in the first few centuries, have always appealed to *oikonomia*, that is, an application of moral principles and laws according to the salvific distribution of God's mercy. If it can be shown that the first marriage was hopelessly destroyed, if the abandoned spouse had no hope of a reconciliation and could not live as a celibate for the heavenly kingdom without suffering great harm, then they would tolerate a second marriage. Such a marriage was not accorded a celebration because it was not reason for rejoicing but, rather, it was blessed in the form of a penitential service with the assurance of divine forgiveness. At times, the local churches expressed their reservations by excluding from the sacraments for a thirty-day period the separated spouses who had remarried.

At the Council of Trent, a large number of bishops wanted to condemn explicitly this more merciful practice of the Oriental Churches, but the representatives and bishops of the republic of Venice intervened. Venice controlled a number of dioceses in the Orient where Catholics and Orthodox lived side by side under the authority of a Latin bishop and they knew about the Orthodox tradition. After prolonged discussion it was decided that while condemning a Protestant position that asserted that adultery dissolves the marriage, the Council would defend the practice and doctrine of the Latin Church but would refrain from any overt condemnation of the ancient practice of the Orthodox Churches.

I want to state unambiguously that I adhere to the doctrine of Trent which teaches: "If one should say that the Church erred while she taught and still teaches that according to the evangelical and apostolic doctrine (see Mk. 10; 1 Cor. 7): that the bond of marriage cannot be dissolved because of adultery of the other spouse and that both, including the innocent who has not given occasion to the adultery, cannot remarry during the lifetime of the other spouse; that a man who divorces his adulterous wife and marries another or the wife who divorces the adulterous husband and marries another commits adultery—let him be anathema."[2] The editors of the *Enchiridion symbolorum* assert in a footnote to this

[2] Denziger-Schönmetzer, *Enchiridion symbolorum*, No. 1807.

text that the Greeks were not condemned by this statement since they did not oppose this doctrine of the Latin
Church. Indeed, the doctrine is one that inspires hope
and educates toward hope. Even in the case of adultery,
the innocent party must not be obdurate; he must do
his best to salvage the marriage by generous forgiveness
and, in some cases, by his greater attention to the giving
of more affective and effective love. It would be destruc-
tive of hope to teach that an act of adultery dissolves the
marriage bond, because marriage would then no longer
reflect the Covenant of God with mankind. Even after
greater sins than adultery, God preserves and re-estab-
lishes the Covenant by forgiveness and reconciliation.

The questions posed here are quite different: What can
the Church impose under grave sanction on the abandoned spouse whose marriage is thoroughly destroyed
and dissolved? Must this person remain celibate all his/her
life even when it becomes evident that it is psychologically more harmful to the person and to others than a new
marriage? The question is not whether the Church can
dissolve a God-sanctioned marriage but whether, after
the total destruction of the reality of marriage (not just
after a sin of adultery), the bond of marriage in its con-
tractual reality does absolutely preclude a second marriage.

Biblical scholars generally agree that they cannot prove
either thesis with absolute certainty; however, many
scholars of all Churches are strongly inclined to think
that in this case also, the Bible as a whole calls for a morality that serves the well-being of persons. What could
have been the best solution for all persons involved at a
certain period of history need not necessarily be the most
appropriate solution for a totally different social and cultural context. A study in depth is now going on in the
form of a painstaking research as to what constitutes the

total tradition of the Church in both the East and the West and serious reflection about the possible consequences of various theoretically possible solutions. All Christians should show concern by praying that the Church may arrive at a right solution for millions of people who today find themselves in such difficult situations.

Evidently, the Church cannot fall short of her duty to promote the stability of marriage in absolute fidelity to divine teaching and in readiness to forgive generously. But when all such efforts have been exhausted, the Church has to face the question of showing mercy to those who are divorced or forever abandoned and who, in spite of all their good will, cannot live in celibacy. Is it not possible for the Catholic Church to adopt in a circumspect way a praxis which has been widespread in the East, at least since the second century, and which can be proved to have been in force at least sporadically in the Latin Church until the twelfth century? I have no ready answer to this question. However I consider it a sign of hope that moralists and pastors are losing sleep thinking about the problem while, in compassion and prayer, they seek God's will.

As in a number of previous publications, I am more directly concerned here with those persons whose first marriage has failed and are now living in a second canonically invalid marriage. I am referring specifically to a second marriage that is a stable and humanly speaking harmonious union. Should we try to separate such people, knowing all the while that this would do great harm to them and to their children? Why can we not give the absolution and admit to the eucharist those who responsibly cannot separate and who, in conscience, are convinced that God does not impose on them the hazardous effort of living together as "brother and sister" when this might entail greater moral danger? Only callous rigorists settle the question with a simple response: "After all these people are sinners and so have no right to be admitted to the sacraments." One may ask: Who are the greater sinners, the self-righteous rigorists who look down on the "unclean" or these people who are sorry for their past failures and are now searching truly for God's will?

Many pastors do sympathize with such couples, but they respond in a way that seems to divorce the "sacramental system" from the proclamation of God's mercy. They say: "Of course, you should not doubt that God, in his infinite mercy, forgives you; your repentance for the sins of the past and your sincere good will show that his grace has reached you, but you cannot expect the Church to give this assurance through the sacrament of reconciliation and the partaking of the eucharist." No doubt this attitude is a great step forward compared to that rigorism which simply condemned these people outright and deprived them of any hope without qualm of conscience.

While the Church wrestles with the problem of whether or not she could and should allow remarriage for those abandoned spouses who have no hope of reviving the previous marriage and cannot live in celibacy without great moral hazards, we should at least apply the *internum forum* solutions to those who are living harmoniously in a second marriage and cannot be advised to separate. In the numerous cases in which the previous marriage was most probably never made in heaven, the existing harmonious marriage should enjoy the *favor iuris;* this means that pastors should be warned not to tear asunder what most probably has the blessing of God. In this age when it is so difficult to live a lonely life, should not the fundamental right to marry prevail against a slight probability that the previous marriage was valid? At any rate, if people come to us in all sincerity and good will, we must model our conduct on that of Christ: "All that the Father gives me will come to me, and the man who comes to me I will never turn away" (Jn. 6:37).

The Church must be a true sacrament of Christ, and her sacramental practice must manifest her fidelity to Christ's mercy. There must be no dichotomy between the proclamation of the message of salvation and the sacramental life of the Church. When she is faced with people of good will, the decisive question cannot be whether their marriage situation can be settled according to canon law but rather whether they can be helped according to the principle so classically stated by St. Augustine: "God does not impose impossible things, but by giving his command, he admonishes you to do what you can and to pray for what you cannot do."[3]

The Church of the merciful Samaritan must forcefully contradict the pharisaical attitude of the spouse who, considering himself innocent, would like to consider his marriage non-existent because of an act of adultery on the part of his spouse. It is incumbent on the Church to convert the faithful from loveless judging to merciful reconciliation. She also has to see that her canon law, her explanation of moral principles and her sacramental practice all manifest Christ's basic mission, his coming to heal the contrite. As far as I can see, progress has been made in this direction of blending the call to fidelity with mercy and compassion. The Church is thus becoming more visibly a sacrament of hope.

The growth of this evangelical attitude in the Church is a sign of hope particularly for the evangelization of people in those cultures where Western canon law and casuistry are totally alien and alienating. The same is

[3] Augustine, *De natura et gratia*, cap. 43, CSEL 60, 270.

true with respect to colored people in countries such as the United States. Slaveowners formerly made it impossible for their slaves to have legally recognized marriages. If as priests we judge the colored who are living harmoniously in a second stable marriage according to the dictates of canon law and not according to their own good will, we incriminate ourselves by becoming the accomplices of those who first ruined their family life.

Among many of the African tribes the concept of marriage differs considerably from that of our European and American tradition. While with us marital consent and subsequent physical union together constitute the whole reality of marriage, most African people regard marriage more as a developing reality to be finalized and solemnized only at a later date. They have their own ideas about priorities and moral concepts. When young people come to live together, it is a matter of social responsibility. They have a sincere prospect for marriage; they look forward to a lasting covenant. But there is a period of time during which not only the two spouses but also the two families are involved in observing whether or not it will work out as a stable and happy union. It is only after a serious effort and often after the first child has been born that the tentative partnership becomes an irrevocable marriage. The decisive part of the dowry is handed over and other customary ceremonies take place attesting to the final commitment not only of the two spouses but also of the two clans involved in this marital pact.

To my knowledge, missionaries react to the custom by advising the Christians that the canonical sacramental celebration should coincide with the tribal finalization. In the meantime, however, the young couple looking toward the finalization of their marriage bond are excluded from the sacramental life of the Church at a time when they particularly need it. It hurts them if the practice, deeply rooted in their whole tradition and culture, is regarded as concubinage or living in a proximate occasion of sin. Exclusion from the sacraments and the whole system of discrimination has had no noticeable impact on the practice; it has failed to bring about any change in their customs and serves only as a permanent cause of alienation from the Church.

Two years ago I wrote an article in *Christus* entitled: "Contestation missionnaire de la morale"; the article is now a chapter of my book, *Theology of Protest*, under the title of "The Missionary Dimension of Protest." This article inspired a number of bishops to reconsider their policy. For example, in one diocese these changes were made. The young couple would no longer be excluded from the sacraments provided the following conditions were met: (1) if at the time they came together, they announced the fact to the catechist or to the pastor; (2) if, by affixing their signature to an official document, they expressed their serious intention to finalize the marriage at the proper time, provided there were no grave obstacles; (3) if, in the meantime, they received instruction on how to live a Christian married life and learn to grow in faith and love, praying together. Instead of alienating couples, this new approach helps make this period a kind of novitiate or something similar to temporary vows during the first years of religious life. This is the African way; and under present circumstances, such may well be the only way to bring hope to them, at least until cultural change makes possible a more ideal regulation.

Pastoral mercy can and should give rise to hope, but we need free ourselves from a judgmental attitude that betrays our lack of knowledge about man and his behavior and reflects a static view of morality. Life is growth and as such bears the mark of hope. Therefore we must never try to impose an abstract ideal on people; rather, we should help them orient themselves definitively toward the ideal goal while searching humbly, patiently and courageously for the next possible step in the right direction. Furthermore, knowledge of man's social nature will not permit us to separate individual effort from social reform.

Both in the Church and in the world, only a constant and radical conversion striving toward a synthesis of justice and mercy with personal responsibility and social reform can free mankind from the great temptation of despair and from the many failures to which a lack of hope gives rise.

16

THE COURAGE TO BE

Some time ago, I had the privilege of meeting one of those humble saints whose thoughts were far removed from any dream of canonization by herself or others. The young lady lived with a very refractory husband for seven and one half years. He held four doctorates but in no way could his intellectual ability compensate for his total heartlessness as a husband. He was insensitive to the point of complete sexual impotence. Still, the young woman remained supremely confident that in time she would be able to help him overcome his psychological hurdles, but that hope gradually faded away. She had no trouble obtaining a marriage annulment in the civil courts. When I met her, she had been waiting four years for a similar decision on the part of the ecclesiastical tribunal. She had submitted to the required medical examination to ascertain whether or not the hymen had been perforated; it was found to be intact. The ecclesiastical annulment was finally granted.

As her spiritual guide I found it difficult to contain my own feelings of anger and indignation. Her personal stamina and fortitude had carried her through the ordeal without a nervous collapse. In fact, she was profoundly grateful for the privilege of living with her dear parents, brothers and sisters again. She felt that the Church's formalism was indeed regrettable but she retained peace of mind in the face of the most trying circumstances. The only frustration she ever voiced was that she felt she should have been more generous in pursuing her work helping other people. For many years she had devoted the best of her energies assisting exceptional children; they were an object of great concern for her and she found the work rewarding. She sensed strongly that these children were capable of great affection and gratitude.

I learned a great deal from counseling such a person; she led me to a deeper appreciation of the jarring passage in the Epistle to the Hebrews: Christ "learned obedience in the school of suffering, and, once perfected, became the source of eternal salvation for all who obey him" (Heb. 5:8–9). It is evident that in this context, obedience means the constant acceptance of any personal mission by entrusting ourselves to Christ in faith so that he can manifest the full depth of his love. He is the Divine Master of unselfish love for all who accept to follow him.

As long as we oscillate between optimism and pessimism, we cannot grasp completely the uniqueness of Christian hope; this humble lady exemplified the courage of being Christian in its fullest sense. What sustained her through the many years of constant thwarting and thanklessness was her faith in the Paschal Mystery with its treasure of joy that inspired courage to accept suffering in union with Christ. Her faith reflected the redemptive power of love and the sense of dedication needed to serve the severely handicapped. She accepted the challenges of life in a spirit of thanksgiving.

When we are faced with such biographies, it becomes evident that all optimistic metaphysical systems ring empty and superficial. He who approaches life with the simple enthusiastic expectation that "everything will be all right" is ill-prepared to confront life in its reality. The day will come when all illusions will collapse and there will then be nothing but scorching bitterness. Today's pessimism arises from the superficial optimism that marked the world of yesterday. People tended to expect much more from the world than it could offer or occasionally they expected too little of it. Their expectations and hopes were lacking in depth and they consequently were traumatized when they had to go on living in the midst of so many upsets and disillusionments.

Pessimism turns out to be the most deceitful of all doctrines; it is afraid of suffering. It flees from the battlefield of life and betrays its deepest meaning. Pessimism renounces the fullness of life because it lacks the courage to be. The pessimist is wanting in resoluteness to face reality in depth and to probe all its possibilities, that is, he refuses to learn love in the school of suffering. To know that life brings pain and freely to accept suffering as part of life's total meaning, to understand the significance of suffering not so much as an abstraction as by the courage to be authentically Christian, to come to the actualization of the best of oneself in the midst of trials and frustration —this is what Christian hope does and alone can do.

It is not so much suffering itself as an apparent "senselessness" that makes it so unbearable to many. Man can bear up under the most horrendous sufferings if he discovers some deep meaning in them. This presupposes that man yearns for a total grasp of the significance of life although he may come to this knowledge only gradually and through growing pains. The total meaning of suffering is love that hopes and the hope that discovers gradually the dimensions of true love.

The courage to be and to find one's true self in the

midst of suffering—not only in spite of it but especially by confronting it—manifests the full depth of human freedom. Freedom comes into its own only when it accepts the greatest challenges in life and love. To seek a life on earth in which there will be no more suffering and no more frustration is a coward's way of escaping from freedom's choice and its highest dignity. Freedom grows with our courageous "yes" to the real conditions of life and in full awareness of the complexity of the present situation including its many possibilities and limitations.

Anyone who dares to face his own need for purification knows that suffering can offer the greatest opportunity for freedom. I refer specifically to those sufferings which appear to be the price for justice and peace; they are a test of unselfish love and fidelity in the school of the Divine Master. Enjoying such a freedom, a person can endure suffering not only without being hurt but can even look on it as a royal path to still greater freedom because he has already opted for its saving meaning.

The first Beatitude reminds us of the strength that comes from the acceptance of suffering: "How blest are those who know that they are poor" (Mt. 5:3). Undergirding this Beatitude is the awareness that all good gifts come from God. Included in this notion of poverty is the courage to face one's own unworthiness with trust that God is infinitely good to those who are simple-hearted and humble; he grants them a share of his kingdom.

The high-mettled acceptance of purifying sufferings betokens a sincere yearning to experience the blessedness of those "whose hearts are pure" (Mt. 5:8). It is the courage to be, while sensing the need to become; it implies the resoluteness to come into one's full personality integration by accepting the daily need of further purification and conversion. It is the courage of a sinner to be son of God, knowing full well that one can only be so because of

God's active mercy and patience: "You must endure it as discipline: God is treating you as sons. Can anyone be a son, who is not disciplined by his father? If you escape the discipline in which all sons share, you must be bastards and no true sons" (Heb. 12:7–8). The courage to be a son comes only from God's gracious and undeserved action of purification opening the heart and mind in an existential way to the most hidden Beatitude: "How blest are the sorrowful; they shall find consolation" (Mt. 5:4).

Sin results in the most dangerous and depressing kind of frustration. It has about it all the offensive odor of despair. The idle and self-centered regrets that follow sin strangle the creative energies of hope. They confine man more securely than ever in the helplessness of an imprisoned selfish ego. Sorrow in Christ makes possible a new opening to God, neighbor and true self. Sorrow involves a new acceptance of oneself and one's sufferings. It brings man's failures into the saving love and light of Christ. It reveals an acceptance of suffering in which the power of the Paschal Mystery is operative.

The acceptance of oneself with all one's limitations and failures is not possible without a profound suffering but it is a healing experience. It is precisely sorrow in Christ that leads to a new redemptive acceptance of oneself. It opens up new horizons of being and leads to a more outgoing form of existence. Redemptive suffering with self-acceptance is a condition for the redemptive meaning of all the sufferings which a person will likely encounter on his way toward self-realization in community.

Self-acceptance is a prelude to responsibility, to the courage to bear along with one's own burden a part of the burden of one's neighbor. It prepares us to be increasingly grateful toward those who bear a part of our own burden.

Sorrow in Christ also frees us from self-pity. It means

a sharing in the suffering of the One who came to bear the burdens of all. In the blessed sorrow of a contrite heart, the eyes are opened to the horrifying dimensions of sin as an injustice to God's love and as an obstacle to the salvation of the world. The contrite sinner realizes that each sin is a source of dangerous environmental pollution in which many will have to suffer unless he himself, by suffering, purifies his heart in order to become a source of salvation in his immediate surroundings. But this profound suffering is very much akin to the pangs of childbirth which portend the hope of a new life. It is the prologue to a creative change toward openness in justice and love.

"How blest are you who weep now; you shall laugh" (Lk. 6:21). Blessed are those who opt for purifying suffering instead of the oppressive frustration of self-pity and anger. Blessed are those who, through faith and hope, opt for a right understanding of life while facing its vexations. They will increasingly display the courage to be and the courage to become. They will experience the joy associated with the fullness of a life continually unfolding itself.

The courage to be sustained by Christian hope is not the courage of the healthy, the strong, the righteous, the mighty. Rather, it is the hope of the "hopeless." At no time can we be allowed to forget that the focus of Christian hope lies not in the idea of an open future but on the One who, by the "hopelessness" of his situation on the cross, paved the way to the future. Christian hope gives the courage to be to the poor, to the discriminated against, to the sick and the sinners, to all who put their trust in him. He has saved the world by his cross and thus has opened onto the vista of the resurrection the hope of a new earth and a new heaven, home of justice and peace.

In Christ, the crucified and risen Lord, the kingdom of

God comes to those who acknowledge their personal poverty, to the sick, the discriminated against and the sinners. God's kingdom comes to the sufferers but not through a soothing promise of reward after death. His kingdom is truly here and now, coming in hope to those who entrust themselves to the crucified Lord who chose to range himself with the poor. He refused to adopt the age-old rebellion scheme of the oppressed against the rich and mighty since such a revolt betrays the frustration and envy of those who want to become powerful and wealthy. Christ has humbled himself in the greatest courage of becoming the Servant in order to save all from that temptation to rise above others by using them as steppingstones to one's personal enhancement.

The poor who accept the kingdom of God coming to them in Christ, the Crucified, radically express a new way of protesting against the miserable cowardice of the mighty suppressors, of the righteous and the contemptuous; it is the saving protest of love that calls all to conversion, to brotherhood in Christ. The Crucified summons to solidarity in suffering so as to free all men from the shackles of a meaningless and harmful suffering. He calls to solidarity in justice, peace and love. He gives to his disciples—the poor and those whom the contemptuous view as "hopeless cases"—the courage to be on his side. In Christ, the poor hope, work and suffer for the liberation of the wealthy and mighty oppressors, for the sinners, for the redemption of the self-righteous as well as for their own liberation. The future begins where the righteous are about to be freed from their presumptuous trust in themselves and from their contempt of others, where the mighty are to be liberated from their desire to assert themselves by refusing justice and love to others.

Hope bears the sign of the presence of the One who is our hope when those who were dichotomized into oppressors and the oppressed, into the clean and the unclean people, into the righteous and the sinners, find all together the courage to accept the painful fact that they are poor. Christ, our hope, is with all who find the courage to live with others in the company of him who had the courage to become the Servant of all.

17
HOPE AT ITS SOURCE

In the midst of all his frailties and failures, what constitutes the fountainhead of man's hope? There are many fountains and sources but not all furnish clear water.

Work as an expression of the creative self, especially when performed in the service of humanity, is one means of self-realization. It brings joy and increases a healthy self-trust. But if man works only for self-actualization or devotes all his energies and places all his trust in work, then with each failure his confidence will waver and become subject to re-examination.

There is joy and expectation in study and reflection, in scientific inquiry, especially in the experience of sharing in the process itself and in the results of research. They can contribute greatly to the enrichment of life, but all too often the fragmentation characteristic of modern science and the lag in the implementation of the findings constitute a source of frustration.

Reflection, meditation and dialogue about the great questions of life, faith and revelation serve to undergird life and hope. They demand depth of thought, but we should not tarry on the abstract level where God remains an "it"; the fact that research and speculation so often remain on a theoretical plane can become an insurmountable obstacle to faith in a living God. Theory can degenerate into futile disputes, as it has in the past in the case of theological schools and separated Churches. Even an interior contemplation that only pursues peace of mind cannot totally direct man to God in hope and faith.

With hope, man turns to his innermost depth, where being at home means "being with" and an "outgoing existence"; it is there that man entrusts himself to God. This is the very heart of the process of prayer. Hope attains maturity in adoring love of God and in active love of fellow man, provided this love is rooted in God and leads to a deeper awareness of the presence of God.

Man's own capacities, energies and achievements can be a source of natural optimism but one that is always threatened by misgivings and failings. The more man reaches out toward maturity and the courage to be, the more he becomes aware of his own limitations; this helps create a healthy insecurity in him. There is no other path for the man-come-of-age than this "holy insecurity." It is a life trustfully lived in the presence of God, who alone can give to a frail creature the courage to be and to become in the midst of human insecurity. It means a total reliance on God after we have learned the wholesome way of self-doubt and distrust of the world insofar as this world does not place all its confidence in God.

In prayer, life and hope are at their source, whether it be the prayer of praise and thanksgiving, the prayer of sorrow or the prayer of petition. Thanksgiving brings many to the blessed consciousness that good things are more than material realities because they come from God. They are signs of God's loving presence and care, a constant appeal to us to entrust ourselves to him and to radiate hope by the utilization of his gifts as signs of the

hoped-for solidarity of all men in God. We have referred
earlier to the hopeful character of the prayer of sorrow
which allows even the greatest sinner to have the courage
to be while he experiences the dawning of a creative
transformation.

The prayer of petition reflects hope to the extent that it
expresses or increases absolute trust and confidence in
God. We are assured by faith that God will grant us
whatever we ask in the name of Jesus, that is, increase in
wisdom and love, light and fellowship in the Holy Spirit.
In the prayer of petition the believer knows that God
will grant him more than he is asking for, and he is prepared to receive whatever comes unexpectedly with that
same confidence and trust. "God is a generous giver who
neither refuses nor reproaches anyone. Man must ask in
faith, without a doubt in mind; for the doubter is like a
heaving sea ruffled by the wind" (Jas. 1:5–6).

The Lord himself tells us exactly what we should long
and hope for; he does so in the our Father. Our first
prayerful demand in hope pertains to the courage to live
as children of the one God and Father. It calls for that
courage to believe wholeheartedly that in Christ we not
only bear the name of children, but even on earth we can
hope to honor the name of the one Father by promoting
the brotherhood of men. It implies a resoluteness to do so
patiently, knowing full well that final and complete manifestation awaits the end of history.

Prayer introduces us to the salvific tension between the
"already" and the "not yet," thus turning us into untiring
pilgrims. It does not allow us to dream of a perfect anticipation of the heavenly mode of dwelling in God's love
nor does it allow us to look lazily at the skies. When our
prayer is sincere, we set out with God's grace toward the
heavenly way of doing God's will, that is, in a spirit of

praise and thanksgiving and in full solidarity with all of God's children and his creation.

When we kneel before God in prayer, we learn that it is not permissible to long and hope merely for one's own bread; prayer extends our hope to all men so that they may learn to share their bread, co-ordinate their skills and utilize their organizational talents to feed all men. Before God, we realize that men not only crave for money and nourishment for their body. To eat our bread together means acknowledging effectively the dignity and freedom of all men and allowing them an active part, a real co-responsibility in economic, cultural, political and international life.

When praying for our own needs, we realize more and more how the sharing of our daily bread takes place at the common table of life. In partaking together of the Word of God and of the eucharistic bread, we realize that we can effectively hope for the heavenly banquet only in that solidarity of hope with which our whole life says "Our Father." It is through prayer that we come to an ever-fuller realization of how we should hope for peace and reconciliation. We are "sacred liars," i.e., we are uttering unholy lies using sacred words when we hope for the gift of shalom without evincing any willingness to be peace-makers. It is through prayer that we come to the existential understanding that we cannot escape the dark powers in our own heart and our environment unless we commit ourselves simultaneously to the purification of our own self and to the building up of a divine milieu of goodness, kindness, sincerity, purity and justice.

Prayer is hope in operation, because it is hope at the very source of all creative and redemptive action. Being at home in God's loving design means being a part of his promises for the world. Thus we become bridges of hope capable of spanning the gap between faith and life. If our hope in prayer is truly Christian, the whole world in us, with us and through us attains the source of its hope since we hope and pray for the well-being and salvation of the whole world.

Prayer is hope at its source only if it follows the prophetic tradition that excludes any dichotomy between religion and life, between faith and hope, between love of God and love of neighbor. Formalism is one of the greatest threats to prayer and hope. Of course, some structure is needed for our common celebrations and prayer, but there must always be room for spontaneity and creativity. The whole style of prayer must allow freedom to the Spirit who renews the face of the earth.

Prayer is hope in action only if it follows the Word Incarnate and therefore in no way inclines toward a Hellenistic concept of contemplation which tries to escape reality and commitment to the visible world. The prayer of active hope makes man a sharer of God's Sabbath (-repose) that gives light, peace and direction to his creative presence in the world.

Prophetic prayer arises from experiencing solidarity with sufferers, the poor, the discriminated against, the oppressed; it offers this vital solidarity to God in Jesus Christ to be strengthened and deepened. Thus does hope at its very source make the believer an ever more effective sign, a "sacrament" of hope for the world. The more hope remains at its source through a genuinely prophetic prayer, the more the messengers of hope can bring a sense of wholeness to life, integrate the expectation of the final coming of the Lord and his coming in daily events and synthesize hope for "the new earth and the new heaven" with commitment to a better world in which man can live while on earth.

As far as we men are concerned, hope at its source gives God freedom to be everything in all things. In prayer we commit ourselves in trust to God granting him a free hand to remove all obstacles to the fulfillment of his promises.

Hope in action, an active trust that fosters hope in our neighbors and in the world around us, is prayer whenever two are gathered in the name of Christ. In full awareness, they consent in word and in deed to that solidarity which is the sign that they are at the source of hope in God.

Illiterate Russian peasants have communicated this truth to me in a most forceful and hope-inspiring way. When, after the battle of Stalingrad, in an effort to escape captivity along with sixteen gravely wounded and sick men, I arrived alone at the house of a poor Russian family, we were taken in as cordially as if these people had received Christ himself. The family sheltered us in spite of the grave dangers involved; the highway on which the Russian army kept moving back and forth was very near.

These poor Russians fed the hungry men and cared for them through the night. This was the most secular language about God but his name was not mentioned. Before leaving I asked what could have motivated them to such a courageous manifestation of love to enemies of their country. The mother of the household replied with the greatest simplicity: "We have four of our sons in the Russian army and each day we pray that God will bring them home safe and sound. How could we go on praying if today we had overlooked the fact that your mother, your father and your friends are praying to the same God for the very same thing?" This is the prayer of hope in action.

Forms of prayer or better still, "prayers" that do not bear fruit for the life of the world are not truly "hope at its source"; rather, they are expressions of man's self-made religion. Similarly, action that does not strengthen an awareness of God's presence in the world is not hope coming from its source. It may even lead away from him who alone is the hope of the world.

The fast-growing House of Prayer movement aims at a prophetic synthesis, the integration of prayer and life, hope at its source and hope in action, the courage to be in the world trusting in God and the confidence that we are bringing hope closer to the world when we turn totally to God.